In *Is This My* Life? *San Miguel and Beyond,* Cynthia Claus gives us an up-close and personal look at her life in San Miguel de Allende and her travels in Mexico. From Palenque with its rich history to Uruapan and its craft festival, readers are treated to the Mexico that those of us who live here know and love. And in San Miguel, whether it is the blowing up of Judas on Easter, veterinarians who sell cast-iron skillets, or the virtues of learning patience, readers will learn that the answer to the question "Is this my life?" is a resounding "Thank goodness, yes!"

    —Carol Merchasin,
    author of *This is Mexico:*
    Tales of Culture and Other Complications

Is This My *Life?*

SAN MIGUEL & BEYOND...

Cynthia Claus

"…everything you notice is important.

Let me say that a different way:

If you notice something, it's because it's important.

But what you notice depends on what you allow yourself to notice

and that depends on what you feel authorized, permitted to notice

in a world where we're trained to disregard our perceptions."

Several Short Sentences about Writing,

Verlyn Klinkenborg

Is This My *Life?*

SAN MIGUEL & BEYOND...

Cynthia Claus

PASHMINA PRESS

Printed in United States of America
First Printing, 2022

ISBN 979-8746810144

Pashmina Press
1900 J F Kennedy Blvd.
Philadelphia, Pa. 19130, USA

www.cynthiaclaus.com

10 9 8 7 6 5 4 3 2 1

Cover and frontispiece photos by Jayne A. Halley
Interior photos: The author, with additional photos from her archives
Book and cover design by Margot Boland

DEDICATION

*Alexander Joseph Robson, 1938-2021, with his then wife-to-be, Cheryl Ruth,
in San Miguel de Allende, Mexico, in 2012.*

*Alex, whom I met when I first came to San Miguel de Allende in 2009 and who became
a treasured friend, was born in England. After attending medical school at Guys College,
he moved to Israel, where, as a surgeon, he performed kidney transplants. There, he met his
first wife, Miri, and their first son was born. He took a* locum *(a temporary position for
another doctor) in Alberta, Canada, in 1973, and loved it so much that he and his family
moved to Fort Saskatchewan, Alberta, where they lived until 1976 and had their second
son. Private practice followed in Edmonton for 32 years, followed by a stint at a clinic in
Fort Saskatchewan. Alex and Miri were divorced in 1995.*

*Alex and Cheryl had known each other from the neighborhood in Edmonton where
their children went to the same school. Years later, when they re-met, he was still doing
triathlons, playing duplicate bridge, working full time, and studying Spanish. After a five-
year courtship, they married in 2014. Travel was a large part of their life; winters were
spent in San Miguel. They moved to Vancouver, as Alex had planned to practice there, but
shortly thereafter his health began to decline. He retired in 2015. He spent the last nearly
three years of his life at an excellent long-term care residence there.*

*Of course, I knew none of this when I met Alex. As I wrote in my earlier book in this
series,* A Lifetime to Get Here: San Miguel de Allende, *"I decided to sample Conver-
sations with Friends, a free, informal program at the biblioteca in which locals…and visitors…come together twice a week to talk…. Since I was a little early and spotted another
expat, I struck up a conversation. Alex and I spoke in English until the time came to speak
in Spanish, and we just continued our conversation. We found we had much in common….
We were both renting here for two months; we had each lost a parent to Alzheimer's; and
our level of proficiency in Spanish seemed identical."*

*Alex introduced me to his Spanish teacher, Carlos, who continues to this day as my
private tutor. And he introduced me to Cheryl, the woman who became his second wife.
What a gift that was, as Cheryl and I continue to be good friends.*

*It pained me terribly to see Alex's slow diminishment from the vibrant, fiercely intel-
ligent, and witty person that he was. It so reminded me of the descent into Alzheimer's of
my father, also a doctor and with those similar personality traits.*

Rest in peace, Alex.
You and San Miguel will always be mingled together happily in my heart.

ABOUT THIS BOOK

I n her earlier title in this two-book series, *A Lifetime to Get Here: San Miguel de Allende,* Cynthia mined her blog posts about being a visitor in San Miguel for longer and longer periods of time and in all seasons over a four-year period, 2009-2012, to offer the honest views of an older, single woman navigating on her own a country new to her. In this second book, *Is This My* Life? *San Miguel and Beyond,* Cynthia, having sold her home in Philadelphia, tells of her life as an almost full-time *residente permanente,* presenting anecdotes about her experiences and situations—both wildly humorous and deeply emotional—told in a relaxed, intimate, conversational style, brimming with lavish details.

The "Beyond" part encompasses short, small-group adventures to such diverse places as the southern state of Chiapas, which borders Guatemala, and Uruapan, the second-largest city in the state of Michoacán, plus an eco-journey to the state of Hidalgo in central Mexico, north of Mexico City.

Cynthia's love for Mexico and all things Mexican, and San Miguel especially, shines through in each of her stories, whether she's complaining about minor difficulties, breathlessly telling a gripping story, or laughing at herself over the linguistic or cultural errors that she makes. You, too, will come to love San Miguel and Mexico when you read this engaging book.

PROLOGUE

The book that you hold in your hands is the second of a two-volume series about living in San Miguel de Allende (SMA), Mexico, for more than a decade. The first title, *A Lifetime to Get Here: San Miguel de Allende* (2020), covers the time period 2009-2012, when I visited San Miguel mostly during the winter, adding other seasons as time went on and staying for longer and longer periods of time. This book, which covers 2013 to the present, tells of living almost full time in SMA as a *residente permanente*. While either book can stand alone, I think readers will get a more rounded view of the many aspects of the city and my participation in it if the books are read in the order they were lived and published.

❀ ❀ ❀

Because I'm a person who is all about stories and sharing them, one of the things I love best about San Miguel de Allende is that almost everything is story-worthy. Even the title of this book has a story behind it.

Pro Música is a nonprofit organization in San Miguel that, from October through March each year, invites some of the world's best classical musicians to perform concerts in the sanctuary of St. Paul's Episcopal Church with its nearly perfect acoustics. It also brings music instruction to a number of desperately poor local *campo* (rural) schools, where there is not even running water. The school program is called "Rhythm, Rhyme and Reason" and is based on Venezuela's "El Sistema." The original U.S. version of the project of the same name was developed by Tim Hazell, who, before his untimely death in SMA in February 2021, just happened to be the teacher at the schools in this program 44 weeks a year. The program uses instruments from Mexico's ancient past, along with those of world cultures, including guitars that are custom-built for children by an SMA master luthier, made possible by an anonymous donation from one of the patron members.

In 2012, Pro Música added an opera, *Tosca*, to its glittering schedule, to be performed at the historic Angela Peralta Theater, originally conceived as an opera house. A fundraising gala was first offered in 2013. That event was to amass funds to roll out the school program to yet another community, nearby Atotonilco, the following month. My friend Sher and I hurriedly bought tickets. The festivities at the inaugural event started off with a champagne reception, in a room with a magnificent view on the second floor of the hotel that my Unitarian Universalist congregation uses for its Sunday services. Waiter-served hors d'oeuvres were passed. I was introduced to a couple of the singers who were performing in that year's opera selection, *La Boheme* (I had a ticket for the following day's performance). This was a night off from performances, and every artist donated his or her talents to the fundraising effort.

I really hit it off with the wife of one of the singers, a *basso profundo*, and half in Spanish and half in English (her English was flawless, of course), she told me her interesting life story and that of her husband, who was a civil engineer until almost age 30, when he started to train for the opera. He has a most incredible speaking voice, so I cannot imagine that in his upper-middle-class milieu no one noticed the operatic potential of his unique voice.

After the reception, we sat down at beautifully set tables for eight and were entertained by about a dozen of the music students from the Los Ricos school on their instruments, led by their teacher, Tim Hazell. It was emphasized that Pro Música and their teacher had no expectations that these kids would be the next opera diva or musical sensation. The program is to bring the joy of music into their lives and that of their families, to give them a sense of accomplishment and mastery that should serve them well in their other endeavors.

We then had a marvelous four-course meal, served impeccably. At my table were the bass and his wife and two other singers. I mean, what are the chances of Cynthia from Philadelphia rubbing elbows and chatting with some of the elite of the Mexican opera scene in an intimate, relaxed, and totally enjoyable setting? There Sher and I sat in our finest clothes, shoulder to shoulder in conversation with opera stars as real people. At one point, I turned to Sher in disbelief and whispered, "Is this my *life?*" Could I really be living this dream-come-true in Mexico? Well, yes, I could be, and I continue to do so with much gratitude.

After dinner, the incredible vocalists entertained us with arias, and before the final piece, the star of *La Boheme*, Rodrigo Garciarroyo, who originally had the idea of bringing the music program to the impoverished schools and who got Pro Música on board, gave one of the most articulate and heartfelt speeches I've ever heard about a very delicate subject. He said he had spent many years in both Mexico and the U.S., and the principal difference is that in Mexico, everything is about family, and in the U.S., it's all about community. He said that Mexicans help each other very much, but that help extends only as far as their families, whereas the foreigners who come to Mexico, and to SMA in particular, form a new community, and give of their time, treasure, and talent to help people whose names they do not know and whom they will never meet. He said that is an incredible gift that we give and lesson we teach. There was not a dry eye in the house. I've often wondered and really didn't know how the *sanmiguelenses* felt about us, and I'm sure it's not all positive, but his talk made me feel wanted and appreciated and loved by the Mexicans here.

Only in San Miguel. This place is magical. Too bad I didn't find it sooner. But I'm living here now, and I am so grateful to be able to experience what this place has in store for me. I feel joyful every day I'm here.

"THE ONLY REAL VOYAGE OF DISCOVERY...
CONSISTS NOT IN SEEKING NEW LANDSCAPES
BUT IN HAVING NEW EYES, IN SEEING THE UNIVERSE
IN THE EYES OF ANOTHER...."

The Maxims of Marcel Proust,
Marcel Proust

"Sometimes the path through life is winding and offers up untrodden
twists and turns that hint at adventure and spark curiosity.
It asks for a willingness to surrender to the unknown,
to trust the turns without being able to see what's ahead,
and to delight in the myriad of discoveries
that are within reach with each step."

The Reluctant Artist, Karen Kinney

CHAPTER 1

EARLY JANUARY – LATE APRIL, 2013

RETURN TO SAN MIGUEL
WITH A NEW IDENTITY

In the years 2009 to 2012, I visited San Miguel de Allende in the wintertime and early spring, with a couple of stays in late summer and early fall. Near the end of 2012, having come slowly and deliberately to the decision to live in San Miguel almost year-round, I sold my house in Philadelphia. After the Christmas holiday season, I returned to San Miguel to become a residente permanente in El Bajío (the heartland) of Mexico, no longer just a short-term visitor.

Flush with money in the bank from the sale of my home, and no costs anymore to maintain it, I decided that the time had come to explore other places in Mexico. For years, I had heard raves about the group-travel company Vagabundos, led by David Rico, one of the first Jóvenes Adelante scholarship students, and a highly successful one at that, and saw that he was offering a trip to Chiapas in late February 2013. Thus, with great anticipation, I signed up for my very first excursion far afield from the San Miguel area.

OFF TO CHIAPAS!

My adventure in Chiapas, the southernmost state in Mexico, right on the border with Guatemala, actually began long before I boarded the bus for the start of the trip. David Rico had sent all of us travelers dozens of websites about the places we were going to visit. I boned up on all of them and had my appetite seriously whetted. Forty-six of us gathered at the Central de Autobuses at the reasonable hour of 10 a.m. to board a bus with a hand-picked driver, Ruben, for our four-hour drive to the Mexico City airport.

I was lucky to have a totally amiable seatmate, Bobbi, as we kept our selected seats for the entire trip (to enable David to see at a glance who might be missing). Our flight did not leave Mexico City until 5 p.m., but it was good that we had plenty of lead time. We got something to eat and then waited an interminable amount of time in the Interjet line to check in. All was fine with the hour-and-a-half flight that left and arrived on time.

We touched down at the Villahermosa airport, surprisingly not in Chiapas but in the state of Tabasco (which has nothing to do with the hot sauce), just over the border of those two states. We were met by another bus and another carefully selected driver, Noé (Spanish for Noah, the pronunciation of which caused much hilarity as people thought of him as "No Way," and the bus quickly was christened Noah's Ark). Noé was our extremely careful and skilled driver for the entire trip, until he returned us to our exit airport in Tuxtla Gutierrez, the capital city of the state of Chiapas, seven days later.

In Villahermosa, we rode all of about five minutes to our first hotel, the Hilton, right next to the airport. I hated this five-star hotel with all of my heart. I would not recommend it to anyone. I think the only reason we stayed there was that it was very close to the airport. We were there less than 12 hours, only for sleeping before we headed out the following morning. It was corporate, cold, shiny, and sterile. There was nothing to indicate that we were in Mexico. The bathroom fixtures were so slick that I could not figure out how to get hot water nor could I fathom how to turn the lights on and off with the keycard I was given. And I don't even want to tell you about our restaurant experience there. It was so bad that it was the first time in my life that I left absolutely no tip for the waiter.

I did sleep well in my palatial room, though, and we left at 8 the next morning for a two-and-a-half-hour drive to our next destination, Palenque, in the ecological and touristic area of La Cañada. Also staying at the Hilton, and leaving at the same time we were, was one of Tabasco state's professional baseball teams, the Olmecs. In other parts of Mexico, soccer is king, but in the south, where we were, it's nothing but baseball.

While enroute, David read us the choices for a fixed-price brunch at our next hotel, Maya Tulipanes. (We had not had breakfast at the Hilton due to time constraints but were advised to have or bring a little snack if we needed it to tide us over until 10:30.) We ordered on a sheet that was passed around and David called in our order on his cellphone. How did trips such as this ever come off before the use of cellphones? David's was used with great regularity for all manner of reservations, orders, checking on things and people, etc.

It was overcast and quite humid. As we drove, everything looked totally tropical: lush and green, with many bodies of water and banana plantations, all of this the polar opposite of San Miguel.

A beautifully and colorfully painted distinctive Mayan corbel arch greeted us at the entrance to our hotel, again for only one night. There was no doubt from this that we were in Mexico!

As we stepped through the arch, we saw a map of the area painted on the wall. During this trip, we would follow the red line right down the middle of the map from Palenque to San Cristobal de las Casas,

The corbel arch over the entrance to the Maya Tulipanes Hotel.

where we would spend five days and go to several outlying areas for day trips, including one in the Sumidero Canyon, before heading home.

Although there was an outdoor dining room, we had our prearranged "brunch" indoors. (My choice was fish, the first time ever I'd eaten it at 10:30 a.m.)

A bit of information about the Maya, who populated Mesoamerica from before 2500 BCE until the Spanish brought about the fall of the last Maya city in 1697. They did not call themselves the Maya nor did they have a sense of a common identification or any political unity. Their name means "the people of the corn." Part of their creation myth says that they were preceded by the creation and destruction of two peoples, the People of the Clay and the People of the Wood. Since corn and people are mutually dependent, the People of the Corn were considered perfection. The Maya were the only Pre-Columbian civilization to develop a writing system that provided complete expression of the language, thus the only Indigenous people of the Americas with a written history.

The Maya were organized into a series of city-states. They had a 365-day solar calendar; it had 18 months of 20 days each, equaling 360 days, and then there were five "bad" or "nameless" days. This time was considered dangerous because it was believed that the portals between the mortal world and the underworld dissolved, and without boundaries, ill-intended deities could cause disasters. To ward off these evil spirits, the Maya practiced various customs and rituals. In spite of all of the hoopla recently, the Maya never predicted that the world would end on December 21, 2012—it was just the end of one cycle of their calendar, which began 5,000 years ago. A new cycle has now begun.

The Maya had a complex pantheon of deities and practiced human sacrifice. Maize, lime, chile peppers, beans, and squash were the main ingredients of their diet, not so different from today. Most structures were made of limestone, often with corbel arches. They had a distinct class system, but there is no evidence of a priest class.

Within the state of Chiapas, there are 5 million people, 2 million of whom are Maya. They are currently divided into five communities or villages, each with its own language, clothing style, and specialty work, such as raising sheep for wool (sheep are sacred to the Maya and are never eaten), pottery making, and the growing of coffee. Some of the communities allow intermarriage; those that do not are now suffering the results of in-breeding. And Maya are living in places other than Chiapas. In all of Mexico, Guatemala, Belize, and Honduras, about 6 million Maya are alive today.

PALENQUE

When we boarded our bus at noon for Palenque, a UNESCO World Heritage site, we were introduced to our local guide, Patricio Murphy. Yes, that's Patrick Murphy, whose father was an Irish adventurer who came to Chiapas and married a Mexican woman. As was the custom of her time, his mother had only a third-grade education. Patricio's father eventually abandoned his family, which included four children, and returned to Chicago.

I can say without reservation that Patricio made the trip for me. He is highly intelligent and incredibly well educated, and seemingly knows everything about everything. He speaks English, Spanish, two of the Mayan languages spoken in Chiapas, and who knows how many others. He was an obvious favorite with the locals at each place we stopped. Extremely left-leaning, he makes no apologies for his position on the Mexican government and on the horrid treatment—past and present—of the Indigenous peoples. Why does that seem to be so in every country? (As this is being prepared for publication in 2022, I am sorry I must tell you that Patricio died in March 2019, at the age of only 52.)

Patricio Murphy, our guide par excellence.

Palenque, the most studied and written-about of all the Maya sites, is a collection of palaces, temples, and tombs remaining from a Maya city-state that flourished in the seventh and eighth centuries. Its ruins date from 226 BCE to circa 800 CE, the time of the beginning of its decline. Sometime in the mid-eighth century, hostilities broke out with other Maya cities. Palenque's finest ruler was Pakal the Great (sometimes written Pacal, which means "shield"; his title was Lord of the Solar Shield). His rule was from 618 to 683 CE and extended over all of Chiapas and into Tabasco state. He began ruling at age 12. His mother helped him for the next 25 years. It was they who carried Palenque to splendor. He lived to the extraordinary age of 80 and was succeeded by his son. His grandson was the last of the kings of Palenque.

It is not known why the site was abandoned, in 799 CE, but soon thereafter, the jungle took it over, and we were told that what we were going to see represented only about five percent of what is there, that probably 1,000 more structures are still covered by jungle. Most of these are felt to be just residences, and so are not of the same interest and splendor as those that have been uncovered and explored to date.

Because of widespread political collapse in the central Maya region, resulting in internecine warfare and a northward shift of population, by the 900s practically all of the cities in this area were abandoned, except in the Yucatán. Several reasons for this have been floated, one being the lack of rotation of crops. Corn needs direct sun, so slash and burn techniques are used to this day to prepare the areas where corn will be planted. After five or six years of growing corn in the same area, there is nothing left in the soil to nourish the plants. Also, the Maya used wood to burn the limestone to make their buildings, creating an environmental disaster. Other reasons could be water pollution, drought, and illnesses. It takes 500 years to recover an ecosystem. The last kingdom of the Maya collapsed 12 years before Columbus arrived.

The first Spanish explorers arrived in Chiapas in the 16th century, by which time Palenque had been abandoned for several centuries. The first European to visit the site and publish an account was Father Pedro Lorenzo de Nada—in 1567. It was he who gave Palenque its name, which means "fortification" in Spanish.

We were very fortunate to be at Palenque on the day that we were, Patricio told us. Without the cloud cover, it could be scorching hot and humid. The highest average rainfall in all of Mexico is at Palenque, which is in the lowlands of Chiapas and is a little over 600 feet above sea level. Our first stop was at the Archeological Museum of Palenque. The artifacts we saw were all reproductions; the original items that were unearthed are in the Archeological Museum in Mexico City.

Pakal the Great.

We studied a model of the palace—the largest building complex at Palenque—which we were about to see. Located in the center of the ancient city, it was built over a period of 400 years and was used by the Mayan aristocracy for bureaucratic functions, entertainment, and ritualistic ceremonies. The four-story tower was for astronomical observation; they practiced naked-eye astronomy. Within the palace were found numerous baths and saunas, and an aqueduct.

We saw some reproductions of hieroglyphics from the Temple of Inscriptions and learned that through the study of them it was possible to document a dynastic list for the city (the first for any Mayan city); the mythology and ritual practice showed a woman as ruler. Also in the Temple of Inscriptions, we saw in reproduction the excavated tomb of Pakal, with its exquisite and complex carvings. The sarcophagus held the richest collection of jade ever seen in a Mayan tomb.

Patricio offered to take a group up and inside the palace; I was not among them. When I climbed up and more importantly down the pyramid at La Cañada de la Virgen last year just outside of San Miguel, I could barely walk for a week afterward. The steps are incredibly steep and there's nothing to hold on to, and it's pretty scary. That didn't stop many people, though. The climbers came upon a boa constrictor digesting something quite sizable; they had photos to prove it. I was impressed but confirmed in my decision!

What's left of the palace today.

There were other ruins such as this one; you get the idea.

David took the rest of us to see other buildings. On our walk, we saw a tree that is laughingly called the gringo tree, because its "skin" turns red and then peels off, just as a gringo's does when he is out in the sun too long. We also saw the sacred ceiba tree, which, like the sequoia, lives for 2,000 years. It has a cottonlike flower and sap as red as blood. The

Maya represent this tree with a form of cross called the foliated cross (more information and photos later).

We saw the Temples of the Cross group, which included the Temple of the Cross, of the Sun, and of the Foliated Cross.

We visited a ballfield where warring leaders, sitting on the hillocks on either side, had their warriors play games to the death.

When we returned to our hotel, its pool was mighty inviting. Following our fairly grueling day at the Palenque ruins, nearly all of us swam and lounged here quite happily in the humid, warm weather.

SAN CRISTOBAL DE LAS CASAS

The next day, in the rain, we left our lovely hotel and the lowlands at 9 a.m. for the trip through three ecosystems and the homelands of three ethno-linguistic groups to the highlands of San Cristobal. This was the first Spanish colonial city, Ciudad Real (the Royal City), established 1528, which is situated at 6,500 feet above sea level. Strangely enough, in the lowlands, it was the dry season, and yet it was raining.

On the journey, we passed through the middle area between the two extremes. In this transitional area is a cloud forest, a rain forest with pines exclusively. This represents only one percent of the ecosystem. Most of the cloud forest has been exploited, and the protected "El Triumfo" in Chiapas is the only remaining habitat of the quetzal. In pre-Hispanic times, the long tailfeathers of the male quetzal were the most precious commodity. Aztecs traveled as far as Chiapas and Guatemala for these feathers. The Lacandón rain forest is the last remaining one in North America.

We made two stops along the way. The first was at Misol-Ha (Broom of Water), a waterfall that starts 90 feet above an almost circular pool surrounded by tropical vegetation. Parts of the movie *Predator*, starring Arnold Schwarzenegger, were filmed here. Patricio thought it was ironic, as the Governator supposedly doesn't like Mexicans. At this waterfall it was raining steadily. Still, people were game and we walked the sometimes-slippery paths to go behind it.

I think this is the only photo of me from the entire trip.

After about an hour-and-a-half ride, our next stop was Cascadas de Agua Azul, a spectacular series of waterfalls. We stayed there for two hours. The minerals in the water give it its brilliant aqua color. Where water falls on rocks or fallen trees, it encases them in a thick shell-like coating of limestone. It had been raining for several hours, so we were lucky that we could still see the blue tint. Had it rained all night, the water would have been brown. We had been told that it would be possible for us to swim here, but because of the rain, only a few brought their suits and even fewer actually used them.

It takes about 20 minutes to walk all of the trails and to see all of the falls, but by the time we got there, some of the trails had become quite muddy and slick, and one member of our party slipped and got pretty coated. After each had gone as far as he or she felt comfortable, we chose whichever little outdoor restaurant looked appealing and settled in for surprisingly delicious meals.

*Rosie from England was one of those who swam, and this is her towel
from the recent Olympics.*

From there, it was a five-hour bus ride to San Cristobal de las Casas. It got colder and colder as we went up in elevation to the highlands. Our destination city was 1,000 feet higher than San Miguel, which is already pretty darned high at 6,500 feet! We took a break at a rest stop in the town of Ocosingo, where almost everyone ordered hot chocolate.

We arrived in San Cristobal around 7 p.m. and were met at our centrally located hotel, Best Western La Noria, by the owner with a tray full of warming sips of mescal in tiny cups, and a mariachi band. What a welcome!

After checking in, we changed out of the light clothes in which we'd started the day and put on practically winter clothes to brave the very different climate we encountered. Dinner was on our own at any of the myriad of restaurants the city offers. There was no heat in the hotel, and it was very, very cold unless you were under the several blankets provided.

San Cristobal de las Casas, founded in 1528 by Diego Mazariegos, is named for St. Christopher, the patron saint of the town, and also for the first bishop, Bartolomé de las Casas. The bishop was a fervent supporter of the rights of the Indigenous, saying that they had souls and had to be treated equally in the eyes of God. The Indigenous still refer to the city by its Tzotzil and Tzeltal name, Jovel, which is a grass used for thatch. (The closely related Tzotzil and Tzeltal languages are the two most common of the Western Mayan language group dominant in Chiapas.) It was the capital of the state until 1892 and is still considered the cultural capital of Chiapas. Designated a "Pueblo Mágico" in 2003, it was further recognized as "the most magical of the Pueblos Mágicos" by President Felipe Calderón in 2010.

The next morning brought only overcast skies, with no warming sun, so it remained unpleasantly cold and damp the entire day. We soldiered on, starting with a two-hour tour of the city guided by Patricio.

It was clear from the women vendors who surrounded us that Patricio was a special friend of theirs. He told us that he had struck a deal with them: They would have 15 minutes to try to sell us their wares and then they would not do any business while he spoke to us. Patricio told us that the Indigenous in and around San Cristobal didn't want us to take their pictures, as they believed that the camera stole a part of their souls. However, we were invited to take photos of these women, since they were enlightened and didn't believe that.

We were happy to purchase the handmade crafts made by this sweet soul with the captivating smile.

They had beautiful handmade things to sell: belts, hats, *rebozos* (shawls), handbags, and one very clever item that every grandparent in the group immediately signed up for. These were pens encased in woven cotton covers with any name we wanted woven right in. They showed us sample pens with the words "Mexico" and "San Cristobal." We were handed a small notebook, where we printed the names we wanted, and the very next morning at our hotel, they were ready for us to pick up.

As these women stood around displaying and selling their goods, they were constantly crocheting more hats like the one pictured. Their industriousness really impressed me. And their personalities charmed all of us.

Here are some of the things we saw on our city tour with Patricio:

The City Hall, or El Palacio de Gobierno, built in the 19th century.

The Cathedral, completed in 1721, with some finishing touches added in the 20th century.

El Templo de Santo Domingo, with the huge Mercado Municipal right in front, containing mostly stalls selling brightly colored and beautifully made textiles.

Every city and town in Mexico has a *zocalo* (main plaza or square). San Miguel is the only one I've encountered so far that calls its central gathering spot *El Jardín* (the garden). Most contain trees with white-painted lower trunks to discourage insects, a gazebo, and hideously uncomfortable wrought-iron benches; the ones in San Cristobal were no different. There were two pedestrian streets, closed to traffic, which had many bars and restaurants with tables and chairs out on the sidewalk, and lots of shops, too.

We were on our own for the rest of the day to pursue whatever interests we had in the city. From knowledge gained on her previous trip to San Cristobal, my bus seatmate had clued me in to a boutique paper factory in town, Taller Leñateros (The Woodlanders' Workshop), which specialized in handmade paper, silkscreens, block prints, and artist books. After some confusing fits and starts, I located it. I got there just as it was closing for lunch, but a Mexican group was entering for a tour, so I just walked in with them.

Once I got inside, I admitted that I was not with the group. Kindly, instead of turning me out, a worker asked if I'd like to see the gift shop. Why, yes, I certainly would! Believe me, I made it worth his while to miss lunch and staff the shop. I bought a T-shirt and tote bag imprinted with a silk-screened image that enchanted me called "Maya en Bicicleta," plus postcards, greeting cards, little memo pads, and who knows what else to take back as gifts. Little did I know that we had a tour planned in English for the next day (it was not on the original itinerary).

From there, I went to the Museo del Ámbar (Amber Museum), located in the former La Merced monastery. Again, it was very tricky to find, even with a map in hand. When I got there at 3:40 p.m., it was closed for the siesta hours of 2 to 4, common all over Mexico. Since I was very, very cold, I considered ditching the whole thing, but decided I could stomp my feet for 20 minutes. I was glad I waited. San Cristobal is a major producer of amber. I learned a great deal about it from informative and attractive displays and two videos. I also enjoyed the gift shop and ogling the super-expensive jewelry made from some fine specimens of the precious material.

By this time, I was chilled through and through, so I sought out a cute little chocolate shop near our hotel, had a steaming cup of semibitter hot chocolate with a touch of cinnamon, and bought a handmade wooden box with metal hardware filled with my choice of its many different and decadent artisanal chocolates.

The next day, with Patricio, we went to the Casa Na Bolom Museum, situated in an ex-hacienda. Casa Na Bolom means House of the Jaguar. A little background information is necessary here, and this will be an exceptionally brief rendition of the compelling history.

The Lacandón (one of the Maya groups) were the only Indigenous people who were never conquered by the Spanish. The last Spanish armed incursion in the area was in the 1600s. The people fled into the jungle and stayed there without any other contact for 300 years. In 1919, Franz Blom, a Danish archeologist, was sent to Chiapas to explore the rain forest for oil by the company that employed him. In 1928, he made contact with the Lacandón people after centuries of isolation. They had not been contaminated by anything Western.

In the 1940s, Gertrudis (Trudy) Duby found political refuge from the Nazis in Mexico. She met Franz Blom in Ocosingo and immediately fell in love with him. Together they traveled to the jungle, where she photographed the Lacandón people extensively, and for years, they collected tools, crafts, archeological pieces, and clothing related to the Lacandón jungle and people.

In the 1950s, a hacienda from the 1890s in very poor condition became available, and Trudy and Franz bought and rehabilitated it. They opened it to scientists to study the Lacandón. Franz died in 1964 of cirrhosis of the liver, but Trudy lived until 1993. Franz and Trudy's wealth has allowed their home to be maintained as a museum and as a place of continuing study of the Lacandón, and has supported reforestation in the area.

The tranquil patio at Casa Na Bolom.

I consider this photo one of the best of the trip.

For the next stop after the trip to Casa Na Bolom, we had secured an appointment with the founder and head of Taller Leñateros, the paper factory, for a tour in English. It turned out to be way more than a standard tour. We were there for a couple of hours while the self-professed "runaway housewife" from San Francisco, Ambar Past, regaled us with tales of starting up the workshop and using only Indigenous labor, which is still true today. I was fascinated that her name was Ambar in Chiapas. Her last name is a shortened version of a much-longer Polish name.

We met many of her workers and saw their various roles in the making of the unique papers they use to construct books and many other paper items. Ambar was justifiably proud of a book they had published last year of the stories of Indigenous women in Chiapas. Each page had a photo of a woman and her story in both her language and in Spanish, all printed on handmade paper and hand-bound. It won all kinds of international awards. I would have bought a copy, but it was exceedingly expensive—understandably so.

We were then taken into the warehouse, where we got to see and touch many of the workshop's creations. Ambar said most of their successes were the result of hit-and-miss happy accidents.

We concluded the visit with a stop at the gift shop, which had been seriously depleted by my purchases the day before. I was so glad that I had had private, unhurried time in the shop to make my selections. This delightfully cluttered and colorful place was one of the highlights of the trip for me.

Sunday, still cold, but sunny at last, was our day to visit two Tzotzil Indigenous communities nearby, and the first, San Juan Chamula, was another high point, actually in serious contention with the paper factory. San Juan Chamula is the principal town of the Tzotzils, one of the two main groups of Maya in and around San Cristobal, and is the main religious and economic center of the community. We left about 9:30 a.m., and as we drove, Patricio told us the history of the melding of the Indigenous religions with Catholicism into a syncretic religion (a fusion of Western and Indigenous elements). This totally fascinating story is just too long to relate here, but he said the prominence in Mexico of the Virgin of Guadalupe was the best example of the co-mingling of the faiths.

Patricio said that what we were going to witness were ancient rituals by shamans and *curanderos* (traditional native healers) to excise illnesses of the soul, such as sadness, fear, weariness, anguish, and depression, among others, and "evil-eye" afflictions. Then we were given very serious warnings about not taking photos in the church, which could lead to confiscation of the camera, and even arrest and imprisonment. The town enjoys unique autonomous status within Mexico. No outside police or military are allowed in the village. Chamulas have their own police force. Also no hats, headscarves, visors, or caps of any kind could be worn in the church.

Our bus let us off near a cemetery attached to the "old" San Sebastian church (which was actually newer than the present church but had burned about a century ago and was no longer in use), and it was here that I saw the foliated cross, a representation of the holy ceiba tree. The brown natural items everywhere were dead pine needles. The people of San Juan Chamula use pine needles and flower petals extensively in their religious ceremonies because they duplicate the forest, and they suggest infinity: You can't count the stars or pine needles. I also heard that each pine needle represents a person being prayed for.

A foliated cross with knobs on the ends and dried pine needles behind.

Vendors almost overwhelmed us as we got off the bus, mostly children saying in English, "Maybe later," which is undoubtedly what all visitors say when presented with the huge number of items for sale. Then we walked through a phalanx of stalls down to the church and its surrounding plaza; no vendors were in there.

The San Juan Bautista (St. John the Baptist) Church and its surrounding plaza.

Because I was unable to take any photos inside the church, immediately after we left it I sat down in brilliant sun to write about what I'd experienced. Here is that account:

When I entered the church, I instantly burst into tears because I was totally overwhelmed by what I was seeing, hearing, and smelling. There was no altar. There were no pews; instead there were small groups of people kneeling on the floor and there were thousands of candles of every dimension, from birthday cake size to dining room table taper size, and candles in glass jars. Fresh, green pine needles were strewn everywhere on the floor. (Talk about a disaster waiting to happen! No wonder the other church burned.) In areas of varying sizes, the floor was cleared of pine needles to make room for the candles. The bottoms of the candles were dipped in already melted wax, stuck to the marble floor in lines, and then lit. People were praying in front of the candles in their language, some crying openly, even men. A man with a scraping tool and a plastic bag circulated, cleaning up the wax from the spent candles to clear the area for the next ceremony.

There were kids carrying chickens under their arms—in plastic bags with heads peeking out—and shamans with bags of eggs. Priests passed the chickens and the eggs over the body of a person with a spiritual illness to absorb the evil, and then the eggs were thrown into a pit elsewhere. Later, I was told, the chickens were sacrificed to eradicate evil. (I did not see this step.) No one would ever eat the chickens or the eggs as that would involve ingesting evil.

Coca-Cola has a fascinating role in the ceremonies: In the past, the sacred beverage, *Pox* (pronounced "posh," a cane-alcohol beverage containing 38 percent alcohol), was brown and sugary. When Coke came onto the scene in the early 20th century, it was very much like the sacred beverage with value added, as it caused burping, which brought the evil up and out. Coke quickly figured this out and at first gave the product away. On a side note, early Coke was full of cocaine and other addicting ingredients. Now, the shamans sprinkle Coke as part of the ritual.

We noted "disgraced" (covered) saints in glass cases. The story on the saints is that when the "old" church burned, the saints survived. The Western interpretation would be that it was a miracle (we were polled by Patricio); the Indigenous take on the situation was that the saints failed to save the church structure and thus are being punished in the "new" church. For several decades, they were placed with their faces toward the wall, and their hands were chopped off because they had failed to work to save the structure. Eventually, when new cases were made for the resident saints, the old saints got the old cases and were turned back around. New garments covered their lack of hands. All the saints were wearing mirrors on their chests; one explanation is that they are to deflect evil.

There had been two baptisms earlier that day, so the plaza around the church was filled with celebrating families at tables with food and live music. The musicians wore rough white wool belted ponchos and woven hats. Kids were running around being kids.

As I was finishing up the description in my journal, a boy of about 7 or 8 approached me to ask what I was doing, and I told him that I was writing about what I'd seen inside the church since photos were not permitted. He asked me for my pen and some paper. I immediately gave it to him, as I had spares. Then he asked for my whole notebook, but I told him that I couldn't give it to him. Finally, he asked for a peso, and I also refused that. He was not at all insistent and went away.

We returned to our bus at the appointed time, again making our way through the eager vendors. We were now off to San Lorenzo Zinacantán, which means "land of bats" in the Nahuatl language. The people there would look different, we were told, as they had mixed with Aztecs. Flowers are a main motif there, and flower-growing is a major source of revenue for the community. We got as close as we could in our big bus to the women's clothing cooperative we were to visit, and then walked the rest of the way through the community. There we saw a young woman demonstrating the lap loom and inadvertently displaying some of their gorgeous embroidery in her blouse. A *huipil* (traditional blouse worn by Indigenous women from central Mexico to Central America) on display, embroidered front and back, took eight months to complete, we were told.

By then we were pretty hungry and were treated to tacos made from freshly prepared tortillas by a girl probably not yet 10 years old. The tacos were make-your-own, and we got to choose from *chorizo* (a type of pork sausage), beans, red and green salsa, and cheese. Then it was on to their showroom—and let the buying begin!

We again walked through the town to return to our bus, and just before pulling away, the head of the cooperative boarded to thank us in Spanish for coming and welcomed us to return any time. I understood it all!

On the last of our five days in San Cristobal, those who wanted to could visit the cave of Rancho Nuevo, originally owned by a timber company, which, Patricio told us happily, was constantly involved in reforestation. His father was one of the members of the first team to explore the cave in the '60s. Vicente Kramsy, a photographer, was the first non-Indigenous Westerner to "discover" it, in 1965. The Tzotzils, of course, had used it for centuries for ceremonies.

Patricio told us that this team had become addicted to exploring the cave and would spend every free moment in it. Because it was huge— several kilometers long—and had many chambers in which it was easy to get lost, they occasionally came upon skeletons of people who never found their way out. His father's team would draw arrows on the walls in fluorescent paint as they went along to help themselves and others get out safely. He told us a scary but true story about a terrible incident in the cave involving his father, who thankfully did finally get out of the hole he'd fallen into but was found hallucinating after several hours in the dark, alone, waiting for his friends to return with the proper equipment with which to rescue him. That chamber is now called Murphy's Room.

When Patricio was a kid, he revealed, his dad would take him and his brother into the cave and in those days there was no electricity nor "boardwalk," and what would take us 15 minutes took them three to four hours to traverse. I was astonished to learn that a stalactite grows only one centimeter in 100 years!

We spent a little time in a small museum near the cave that had pictures of some of the early explorers, including Patricio's father, and figures dressed in some of the many costumes of the area, including the Zapatistas. In and around San Cristobal, there were many references to them, including photos (in ski mask, as might be expected) of *Subcomandante* Marcos, a Mexican insurgent, the former military leader and spokesman for the Zapatista Army of the National Liberation in the ongoing Chiapas conflict.

Dolls and other souvenirs with Zapatista themes were for sale.

Some lovely stalls outside the cave were selling souvenirs, and I almost missed the bus while buying a bag with an exquisitely embroidered toucan and flowers on it. I know David would not have left without me!

From there we took the Pan-American Highway to a Tzeltal pottery-making village. The potters have to travel four kilometers to dig up the clay, which comes in two colors, red and gray. Again, we had to park the bus in a center square and walk through the village to the home/workshop of the potters we were to visit. In their compound, we immediately saw two ovens they use as kilns and some of many pottery pieces in various stages of completion.

I was amazed at the beautiful clothing this woman was wearing to work with clay, even though it was covered up with an apron.

The creative process is complete here. If this piece were to be sold, it would rest and dry in the sun before going into the kiln and having paint applied.

One delightful woman said she would show us how they make a representative piece, a jaguar. She said she'd do it fast and then destroy it afterward as it would not be of a fine enough quality to sell.

I asked about the many large burlap bags of dried corn in the yard and was told that that was the large family's tortilla makings for an entire year. I inquired about rats eating the corn and was shown the many cats and kittens roaming around.

A couple of people bought some of the finished pieces from the family and then we spent about an hour going on foot to many of the places nearby selling pottery by the side of the road. I'd say we certainly did our part for the economy of Mexico.

We saw some scenes of poverty as we walked away from the pottery demonstration, and I felt that I was seeing the real Mexico. San Miguel de Allende isn't it, much as I love it.

As a final treat for that night, David had gotten us an appointment with Sergio Castro Martinez, who has put together an amazing museum of clothing and accessories from all of the Indigenous groups of the area, on which he is an expert. There was talk that he was a doctor and that in one of the rooms in his place there were dozens of certificates, but it wasn't until after we'd left that I remembered seeing a documentary about him on PBS some years earlier. He specialized in healing severe burns and worked almost exclusively in the Indigenous communities. I remembered him saying on the video that he had found a German ointment that worked exceedingly well to speed the healing of burns. He was and is an incredible humanitarian, devoting his life to helping the Indigenous and to sharing parts of their lives with the outside world. Below is a tiny portion of what it said about him on Wikipedia:

"Sergio Arturo Castro Martinez (born in 1941) resides in San Cristobal de las Casas, Chiapas, Mexico. He is by training an agricultural engineer, teacher, and veterinarian. However, by nature he is a true humanitarian, ethnologist, and polyglot (languages include Spanish, French, Italian, English, Tzotsil, Tzeltal, and Mayan fluently). Sergio has spent more than 45 years helping to build schools, develop water treatment systems, and provide wound care for burn victims for the many Indigenous cultures and Mexican people of Chiapas. He travels daily to the surrounding Indigenous villages and marginalized urban areas to care for the health and social development needs of the underserved."

I have such admiration for this truly humble man.

The good man himself.

This is a display of some of the pieces Sr. Martinez collected or had been given.

Our time in San Cristobal had ended. I must return there, as it has so many more places that I want to visit: the Jade Museum, with pieces from the Olmec, Teotihuacán, Mixtec, Zapotec, Maya, Toltec, and Aztec cultures; the Museum of the History of the City; the Museum of the Popular Cultures of Chiapas; the Maya Medicine Museum; and others.

We left the city the next morning for Chiapa de Corzo, returning again to the lowlands and hot and humid weather. Our bus could get nowhere near our hotel, La Ceiba, so we had been instructed to bring just overnight bags and to leave our big suitcases on the bus. I absolutely loved this hotel in its jungle-y setting. It had a pool, which made us all very happy. But there was no time to use it just then. We were off by foot to a dock on the Grivalja River to take a boat trip in the Sumidero Canyon. It was exceedingly hot, but we were game.

Wearing safety gear in our speed boat, ready for our ride in the Sumidero Canyon.

We were trussed up in life jackets and put into two speedboats, and off we went for about an hour ride to a dockside restaurant where we would eat lunch. The canyon walls rise 1,200 to 1,300 feet. It took 30 million years for the water to carve out the canyon. Take a minute and let that sink in.

We saw some pretty incredible things along the way, including lots of wildlife: vultures, cormorants, herons, snowy egrets, kingfishers, pelicans, ducks, crocodiles, iguanas, and howler monkeys.

We could easily spot this sizable crocodile on the shore.

You cannot imagine how hot and humid it was down in the canyon. Happily, we were traveling at a high rate of speed most of the time, which generated a breeze. When we slowed or stopped to look at something interesting, the air was stifling, plus the smell of diesel fuel almost caused some of us to upchuck, including me.

The magnificent Sumidero Canyon with its high walls on either side.

We saw a not-so-pretty sight of floating plastic bottles and other debris. People are hired to drag the junk out of the river, but they just can't keep up. Patricio said that in the rainy season it was far worse, with huge floating islands of plastic clogging the river. One of the problems, we were told, is that Coca-Cola doesn't give enough of a return on its empty bottles to make it worthwhile for people to collect and redeem them.

We passed a memorial to workers who died during construction on the dam, which was built to generate electricity and completed in the early 1980s. Four dams now generate 30 percent of all the electricity in Mexico, and more will be built. The river became navigable only when the dam was put in. Unfortunately, some caves that contain archeological treasures are now under water.

We rode back in our boats and walked—now very hot and tired—to our lovely hotel and its waiting pool.

The next morning we left that charming place at 10:30 for the Tuxtla Gutierrez airport and our 12:45 flight to Mexico City. We met up again with Ruben and our bus for the ride back to SMA. We stopped at a very nice place for dinner and reached our destination about 8:30 p.m. Then into taxis for most of us, and home sweet home.

It was a very good trip, one that I would recommend to anyone. I will definitely travel with Vagabundos again. I met many lovely people, had incredible experiences, learned more than I ever dreamed possible about so many things, and continued my love affair with Mexico.

LONG WEEKEND TRIP TO URUAPAN
FOR THE PALM SUNDAY ARTISANS' FESTIVAL

Less than a month after my Chiapas trip, an adventure came along because of the misfortune of another, and that makes for a sad beginning. Four San Miguel gringas had planned this three-day weekend trip to experience the Tianguis Artesanal de Domingo de Ramos, the annual Palm Sunday artisans' festival that is the largest in all of Mexico. It brings all manner of craftspeople from around the state of Michoacán to Uruapan, one of the oldest cities in the country, established before the Spaniards arrived. One of the four had a tragic death in her family and so had to go immediately to the States. My friend Linda invited me to take her place.

A little aside here: Linda's and my children had attended a tiny progressive elementary school, Miquon, just outside of Philadelphia, at the same time decades ago. Linda had been the president of the board for part of that time, and although I knew of her, we were not friends then. In 2012, when we were both at the same wedding reception in San Miguel, we rediscovered each other, even though both of us had different last names from those we had while our kids were at Miquon and different-colored hair. We immediately bonded over our shared past, our mutual friends, the bride and groom, and being extremely happy residents of SMA.

At a little before 7 a.m. on the Friday before Palm Sunday, I met Linda, who was to be my roommate in the hotel that had been booked, and the other two roommates, Helena and Nancy, at the bus station in San Miguel. It turned out that I already knew Nancy, as she was in my yoga class and had attended some UU services. We boarded the bus for our three-and-a-half-hour ride to Morelia, in the state of Michoacán.

When we arrived at Morelia, we discovered that our next bus, directly to Uruapan, had just left, and that no others were scheduled in the near future. We checked out the price of engaging a cab for that one-and-a-half-hour ride, and at 180 pesos each (a total of $60 USD) vs. 150 pesos each for the bus that wasn't there, it was no contest. Our driver, Gabriel, a charming, personable young man who spoke excellent English (he had spent eight years in Oregon planting trees, we found out), drove well but fast on the mostly two-lane highways. Since there were four of us, Linda sat in the front seat as she had had recent neck surgery, and I got the seat in the middle of the back over the hump. There were no seat belts for the backseat passengers. This is not at all unusual in Mexico.

It wasn't Gabriel's driving that worried and scared me; it was everyone else's. Since I had, unfortunately, a totally unobscured view of the road, I can't tell you how many drivers I saw pass on a double line or a curve, coming directly at us until the last possible moment, and other death-defying feats. I have long thought that driving laws in Mexico were merely suggestions. Although we arrived safely, we all agreed that, no matter what, we would take a bus back to Morelia from Uruapan on Sunday.

Reservations had been made well in advance at the Victoria Hotel on Calle Cupatitzio in Uruapan via booking.com, and each set of roommates had a confirmation printed out and in-hand, ready to present to the clerk. While throngs of other guests waited to register, the clerk informed us that there were no reservations in our names and that no rooms were available. We all knew that there was to be no leaving. This was the busiest weekend of the year in Uruapan; there were only a few other hotels that we would consider staying in, and they were surely completely booked.

Linda was having none of the "no rooms available" talk. While the three others of us sat nervously to the side, guarding our luggage, Linda insisted that the clerk call the 800 number for booking.com that was on the paperwork, and they confirmed that we indeed had a reservation and re-sent via fax the notification that had been sent to the hotel originally. Magically, rooms became available. (You must understand that this all took about an hour and who knows what out of Linda and the rest of us as we waited.) We insisted on seeing the rooms that we were being offered, and after a great deal of back-and-forth and negotiations, we agreed on two on opposite sides of the second floor. Later in the day,

Linda received a voice message on her cellphone from booking.com, saying that the hotel had overbooked. Surprise, surprise!

Uruapan is a sad little town almost totally taken over by graffiti except in the city center. We were appalled, and in classic type-A gringa fashion, we came up with all sorts of plans for how the town could eradicate the problem. It truly had nothing going for it except the exquisite Parque Naciónal Eduardo Ruiz, filled with waterfalls (more on this later), and this annual festival.

My travel companions, from left, Helena, Nancy, and Linda in the Café Tradicionál.

By this time, it was mid-to-late afternoon, and we were starving. We set out to find a place to have some food. This was easier said than done. Before we left, we had googled restaurants in Uruapan, and the few that had come up were either gone or not findable. We finally came upon the Café Tradicionál de Uruapan about three blocks from the hotel. This place wasn't even on the list from Google! It was extremely attractive, with beautiful wood everywhere. It became our home away from home and also that of many of the other gringos that had come for the weekend and the festival. We met many folks we knew from SMA, either there on their own or with a tour the Lions Club of SMA had organized.

We gratefully had margaritas and a meal, then returned to our rooms to get organized, to read, and to rest. Much later we resurfaced to have some soup (in the same restaurant) and a quick walk through some of the stalls in the artisans' market, not yet officially open.

Each group, representing a city or pueblo in the state, took its turn parading down the street.

Bands accompanied practically every group. Music is such a huge part of life in Mexico.

Saturday morning found us back in the café for breakfast as we eagerly awaited the Parade of the Villages. I liked the slogan for this year's festival, *"Gente Emergente"* (using the word "gente" twice), which means "the people emerging." I had heard there would be around 2,000 craftspeople from hundreds of Indigenous communities in the state parading in their native dress and carrying samples of their crafts, either in normal size or miniaturized for throwing out into the crowd, a la Mardi Gras in New Orleans. The parade began with an official greeting (in Spanish, of course), "Welcome, Brother and Sister Artisans," spelled out on a banner carried by two women.

With the appearance of an incredible float from a guitar-making community on top of a truck, there were some very tense moments. Their huge instrument was too high for the wires in its path. I fully expected that we would see some young men being electrocuted, but using a variety of unusual aids, they got the outsized guitar under the wires and on its way, although there were other wires to negotiate all along the parade route.

We all held our collective breath until the guitar float negotiated the overhead wires that impeded its progress down the parade route.

As we were having breakfast, we saw this man running up the street to the start of the parade, with his display of hand-embroidered cloths and poles under his arm, so we were particularly happy to see him again in full regalia, strutting his stuff.

Some bystanders twirled wooden noisemakers to herald the arrival of each succeeding group. I particularly liked the name of the town that was next up in the parade, Tzintzuntzan. Writes Judith Gille in her book *The View from Casa Chepitos:* "The word *tzintzuntzan*, when spoken rapidly and correctly [tsin-tsoon-tsahn], is onomatopoeic for the sound of hummingbird wings in flight. In the pre-Hispanic era, the village of Tzintzuntzan was known as the place of the hummingbirds…"

Mexicans seem to me to have a very different relationship with danger than we do up north. (Refer to lack of seat belts and description of harrowing taxi ride, above, for example.) One of the floats in the parade was from a community that does copper work, which requires using a fire. So, naturally, their float had an open fire, and workers were pounding heated copper for all to see. On the float were a thatched roof and paper and cloth decorations. You do perceive the danger of riding down the street in such a float, right? I certainly do. Obviously, in this case, the artisans didn't. On closer examination, I did see two large plastic containers, hopefully filled with water. But still…

At the end of the parade, the onlookers, including us, got in line behind the final participants and followed them to the tented stalls in the central plaza where all of their creative labors for the past year were on display and for sale. The items were of varying quality and price. We spent about an hour and a half there, each going her own way to explore what interested her, seeing only the tiniest fraction of what was available. Another tidbit I learned from reading *The View from Casa Chepitos* is that, thanks to 16th-century Spanish bishop Vasco de Quiroga, who taught self-government, various trades, and handicraft production to the Indigenous people of Michoacán—each village learning a different skill—they became self-sufficient. Now, nearly five centuries later, village artisans still produce the same handicrafts once fabricated by their ancestors.

One of the finer pieces.

There were thousands of pots, plates, baskets, spoons, chairs, musical instruments—really, you cannot believe the volume of products. It was quite overwhelming.

This is my favorite photo from the weekend, as this little girl, deep into her own world, shares her tortilla with the pigeons.

We met up to go to a trout restaurant we'd heard of on the edge of the city. Needless to say, we all had trout, in various forms, but the service was poor and the food only middling. But just outside of the trout restaurant were two delightful, attractive teenage girls handing out samples of *paletas* (little shovels)—like Popsicle ice pops. They chopped up an avocado-flavored one and we tasted it and went wild. Then we sampled the macadamia nut one, and all of us ordered that one, though we agreed that it was a tough choice. They had other flavors as well. I think this was a small, artisanal effort, and we were blown away. We found out that the Uruapan area was a major producer of macadamia nuts as well as farmed trout. Coffee, too.

From there we walked several blocks to the national park, thinking we'd walk off the meal and the unexpected dessert, but by that time it was 4 p.m. and the park was closing in an hour. We decided to wait until the next day, when we could really give it its due.

There had been a *concurso*, a competition where judges selected the best of the best in each category of craft, with cash prizes, and the winners were all on display in La Casa de la Cultura.

One of the magnificent carved wooden pieces that had garnered a prize.

On Sunday, it was back to our favorite restaurant for breakfast. Then, although we had been told it was closed on Sundays, we went to see an old textile factory that was built in the 1870s. Because it was a special Sunday, it was open and we were thrilled. We met the 90-something-year-old gringa who had purchased it with her husband in the 1950s. Of all things, the very day that we were hearing her story was the fourth anniversary of his death. She is still running it as a textile factory, although using only a small portion of it. It had a lovely gift shop featuring products made on-site. Another huge room was being used for an art exhibit.

We walked back into the center of the city and found a shady place to watch the Palm Sunday procession, which we found small and somewhat desultory. After that it was more time in the market. I bought a small lacquered wooden jewelry box, which is something I really needed, but it was so crowded and hot under the tents that we all felt claustrophobic and had to leave.

The charming flower-bedecked entranceway to the hotel's restaurant.

For our final meal, we went to a restaurant in the five-star Hotel Mansion del Cupatitzio, just across the street from the trout place we'd been to the day before. Here, we had a most attentive waiter and totally delicious food in a charming ambiance. I really couldn't figure out what such a hotel/restaurant, complete with extensive and impressive gardens and a pool, was doing in this lackluster town. It appeared to be a site for destination weddings, and we saw the bride and groom for one of them while we were there.

Even after our sumptuous meal, we all hoped for another paleta for dessert, but, alas, the little stand was closed. We were so disappointed. We walked to the park again, paid our admission, and spent several relaxing hours there. This park was a respite and refuge from the graffiti-scarred city and the throngs of tourists in town for the fair. It was spectacular and filled with both natural and man-made waterfalls. Water was everywhere, frequently surprising us, and it was such a nice change from San Miguel, which is incredibly dry.

I loved this water feature with hundreds of tiny, individual falls!

There were lots of places to eat, and on the grounds of the park was a trout farm. We could see it from way above, but I don't think it was open to the public. Naturally, trout was the main menu item at the many stands.

This sign says that in The Little Fish restaurant,
rainbow trout (la trucha arcoiris) is prepared. It also serves gorditas
("little fat ones," a type of stuffed sandwich) and quesadillas.

Available for dessert were fruits cut into rose shapes and put on a stick (and probably dipped in a bit of chile powder for good measure), or just cut into cubes.

This was a wonderful, relaxing, cooling experience—to be in so

Trout being cooked on a comal.

much green, and surrounded by volumes of water, hearing it, touching it. We left reluctantly. Then it was back to our hotel, where we had stored our luggage when we checked out earlier. We took a taxi to the bus station and got our bus without a problem. We changed buses in Morelia, and arrived back in SMA in the dark, tired but happy and fulfilled by our weekend excursion.

AN AUDUBON ECO-JOURNEY TO HIDALGO, MEXICO: WATCHING BIRDS, VISITING PUEBLOS MÁGICOS AND HISTORIC MINES, AND VIEWING NATURAL WONDERS

Spurred on by my wonderful experiences on the Vagabundos group trip to Chiapas, I decided to try another small-group travel experience, an Eco-Journey, sponsored by the Audubon Society in Mexico. Although I am not a rabid bird-watcher, I do enjoy being outdoors, hiking, and seeing nature, and with the help of the leader of this tour, I got to see many birds close up and really got excited about the hobby.

I had a surprise when a huge Mercedes Benz van drove up to the meeting site at 6:45 a.m. and the first person out of the van to join me was someone that I had met some years ago in the jardín, the tour guide, Rodrigo. But then, that's so San Miguel. Rodrigo called me by name, gave me a big hug, and introduced me to his wife, Carmen, and our driver, Juanito, who had come from Querétaro, over an hour away, to bring us our transportation for the trip.

This was my first Eco-Journey sponsored by La Sociedad de Audubon, the only chapter of the Audubon Society in Mexico, and celebrating its 45th year. Its tagline, "Nature and Culture, a Perfect Combination," summed up what I love and was seeking from this trip to the small, mountainous state of Hidalgo, located southeast of San Miguel de Allende, which is in the larger state of Guanajuato. (If you're familiar with the area, it's approximately the same distance from San Miguel to Mexico City—four hours, *más o menos*—as to our first destination, the Pueblo Mágico of Huasca de Ocampo, a short drive from Pachuca, the capital of Hidalgo. Because of its close proximity to Mexico City, there are lots of weekend tourists there.)

Two separate mountain ranges, with pine, cedar, and holm oak forests, present excellent opportunities for hiking and bird-watching. In fact, the area has about the widest variety of wild birds anywhere in Mexico, including eagles, hummingbirds, falcons, and wild turkeys, not to mention 31 species of serpents, and mammals such as skunks, spider monkeys, wild boars, anteaters, and gray foxes.

The three other travelers, Arlena and Judy, year-round San Miguel residents with their respective husbands who did not accompany them on this trip, and Kevin, Judy's visiting brother, made up our very intimate group. Four was the minimum needed for the trip to go, and we had just made it. Most of the Audubon trips have many more sign-ups—although they are always kept small —but by mid-April, most of the "snowbirds" have flown back to the U.S. or Canada, so this was it. There were a total of seven of us in a luxurious 19-passenger van, which included a flat-screen TV. As we stowed our gear, got on the road, and were given the first of many bottles of water, Rodrigo asked if, to pass the driving time, we'd like to see some documentaries about Mexico, and we all did.

Because the trip had started at such an early hour, we were given breakfast sandwiches that we had chosen online the day before, scones, and apples. I happily munched mine while watching an extraordinary film called *The Royal Tour*, which featured Felipe Calderón, while he was still president of Mexico, along with his wife, a two-term senator, and their three children, as they hosted Peter Greenberg of PBS on a whirlwind tour of the country.

They went to Jalisco; Morelia (the president's home city); Baja to see the migrating and calving whales (I want to go!); Michoacán for the migrating monarch butterflies; Chiapas for the Mayan culture; and others I can't remember, all at breakneck speed. They explored caves and swam in *cenotes* (natural sinkholes resulting from the collapse of limestone bedrock that exposes groundwater). They rode on zip lines. I was mightily impressed with President Calderon's spirit, friendliness, and relaxed attitude. I could only imagine what went into making all of those adventures happen in a very short period of time for a head of state, his family, and a guest.

We made a pit stop after only an hour and a half because the traffic was just horrendous on a superhighway, with more trucks than I'd ever seen at one time. As soon as we came to a stop, a young man sprang into action, washing all of the windows. He was not an employee of the gas station but a freelance worker. Juanito gave him a tip. Reminded me of the squeegee guys in NYC.

The second documentary was called *Blossoms of Fire*, about the town of Juchitán on an isthmus between the Gulf of Mexico and the Pacific Ocean in the state of Oaxaca, where matriarchy is practiced. While the movie was underway we were asked to stop at a checkpoint by the *federales* (federal soldiers). Rodrigo told us not to say anything if they came on board. There was a bit of panic when Rodrigo asked us if we all had our passports, and some didn't. Only Juanito got out of the van. The soldiers merely looked us over from outside and asked where we were headed. When Rodrigo told them, their response was "Why so far?" We got a good laugh out of that as we were waved away, much relieved.

We got onto another highway, Arco Norte—new and charging a toll, where there was much less traffic. We drove through Pachuca, which had been a mining town in the past. After the war for independence, when the Spaniards were no longer running the mining operations, a company from Cornwall, England, took over, and although it was there for only 25 years, its influence is still very much in evidence today all over the area. Houses, which look as if they were in the Swiss Alps or perhaps in Cornwall (I couldn't say, as I've never been there) rather than in Mexico, are painted in pastels, and the traditional flaky Cornish *pastes*, "miners' enchiladas," are sold everywhere. Pronounced pasties—two syllables, please—they are a baked short-crust pastry, typically with a filling of meat and vegetables (singular: pasty).

The Cornish miners are much beloved in this part of Mexico. We learned of the Great Trek of 1825, when the miners went from the beach at Mocambo, Veracruz, hundreds of miles overland, carrying 1,500 tons of equipment, to revive the defunct silver mines.

We checked into our first hotel, in Huasca de Ocampo, just in time for a late lunch. Unfortunately, it was much too cold to eat outside on its charming patio. It had been very hot when we left San Miguel, and weather.com predicted 70s and 80s for the region we were visiting. However, it was heavily overcast and drizzling, and we were at nearly 9,000 feet. This town is one of the highest inhabited places in Mexico. While the waiters put the food out, we took a quick tour of the market and a peek into the church there.

In a modest-sized church stood a small statue of a very interesting saint, San Charbel, surrounded by different-colored ribbons with words written on them. I learned later from my Spanish teacher that the ribbons' colors have significance. San Charbel, originally Charbel Makhluf, was born in Lebanon and became a Maronite monk and priest. He lived as a hermit for more than half his life. As a canonized Catholic saint, he is prayed to in matters of world peace, in addition to more personal concerns.

San Charbel surrounded by his meaningful, multicolored ribbons.

We returned to the hotel to eat inside, choosing what we liked from a buffet.

Here's our crew, minus Juanito, in front of our hotel, Casa Azul. (photo by Carmen)

After the lunch and a short time to get settled in, we were off to see the *prismas basálticos* (basalt "prisms"), which are a result of lava cooling very slowly. Rodrigo warned us that the owner of the site had put in a water park right next to the natural wonder, so we were to shut our eyes to that and concentrate solely on the unique formations. Because of the cool weather, only one or two brave teenage boys were in the water.

It was my first time seeing these unusual natural formations, prismas basálticos.

I cannot believe that I walked across this suspension bridge over a deep chasm.
It is so not my favorite thing to do. Happily, there was another way back that did
not include re-crossing it.

From there we visited ex-Hacienda Santa Maria Regla, which was owned by a Spaniard, Pedro Romero de Terreros. In the mid-1700s, when he founded the town and built the hacienda, he was the richest man in the world. This was not a place to live, but was used only for smelting silver, gold, and other metals brought over from the mines in Pachuca. Sr. Terreros lived nearby in another hacienda, San Miguel Regla. The smelting hacienda was located here because of the rich abundance of natural materials for building, plus bountiful water, which was needed to process the minerals. Sr. Terreros paid tribute to the King of Spain, Charles III, in the form of some of the processed minerals, and for this, he was named Count of Santa Maria Regla. He used the Indigenous population as slaves to produce the gold and silver; thousands died, as they were viewed as completely disposable. The only food they were given was rice and beans.

Note well the shape of these formations; you will see them later in a most surprising use.

A Spanish-speaking guide led us through the ex-hacienda and explained the separation process, translated for us by Rodrigo. I have always loved the look of stones and took many photos of them here. As we were having our tour, scores of workers were setting up for a huge wedding the following day, Saturday. While there was no denying the magnificence of the setting, I didn't think that I would want my wedding celebrated in a place that had seen so much human misery.

This is just inside the entrance to the smelting hacienda.

As I've come to expect, there was a chapel on the grounds. The original chapel door, made from ebony, showed almost no signs of its nearly 300 years of use. It was unclear to us if the wedding would take place inside.

I asked you on the opposite page to take note of the shape of the prisms. Here they are used to construct a wall. They were not sliced and added to the building material. What you are seeing are the ends of the prisms, thus the walls were as thick as their length!

We returned to our hotel and enjoyed dinner together, including Juanito, our driver—and that was very important to me. I've been on trips where the driver, and sometimes even the guide, sat at a separate table from the travelers, and I found this disturbing. Juanito and Kevin really hit it off and we all enjoyed one another's company, some in Spanish, and some in English.

The following day, Saturday, those of us who were going bird-watching got up early, had coffee or hot chocolate and sweet rolls, and took off for a Biosphere Reserve. In about three hours we saw many birds and some frogs. Rodrigo is the perfect tour guide for an Audubon trip, as in addition to his great organizational skills and his friendly, easygoing manner, he had the most amazing abilities at bird-watching I've ever seen. He knew the names of all the birds in both Spanish and English, could identify most of them just by their call, carried several bird books with him to check on details, and could spot things most of us couldn't see until he pointed them out. He carried a scope and would set it up and invite us to see what he had seen. It was an incredibly peaceful time near a rural lake with water flowing in ditches by the side of the road. I saw my very first vermillion flycatcher; I have to admit, it was a thrill. I had heard about it for years but had never spotted one. We bird-watchers returned to the hotel and all had a big, late breakfast together.

Some very non-Mexican-looking pastries, a throwback to the Cornish miners' days, laid out on a tartan tablecloth.

Next stop: Real del Monte, another Pueblo Mágico, which, on a Saturday, was very busy with tourists. Driving through there and parking with the huge van were real challenges, but Juanito was up to the task. Rodrigo told us that the very first game of soccer played in Mexico took place in this town, introduced by the Cornish miners. You'll see the Cornish influence in the architecture here. We learned that any buildings that were made of bricks were constructed after the Cornish came to town, as they brought that technology with them.

It being a weekend in a Pueblo Mágico, there was street entertainment for the tourists. A ghoulish fellow was the MC, and the entertainment was live music with scantily clad, beautiful young women dancing, not at all what I expected.

In true Mexican three-ring-circus style, this was all going on right next door to a church that was hosting a wedding. I would have been pretty upset if during my wedding ceremony, drums and other instruments were being played loudly right next door. As the guests came out of the church after the ceremony, they stopped to check out the dancing girls before going on to the reception.

The Cornish miners also introduced Methodism to Mexico. We saw the first Methodist church in the country. The wording over the door translated as Our Methodist Church of Mexico, R.A. (Religious Association)–Emmanuel. What a stark contrast to the Catholic churches in Mexico!

The first Methodist church in Mexico—plain, plain, plain.

Several of our group loaded up on pastes in a variety of flavors to eat at a later time. Believe it or not, I never did taste a pasty, as when I was offered some, I wasn't hungry.

From there we went to the Acosta Mining Museum. Our guide was a miner's daughter. She told us that her father had died at the age of 38, leaving his pregnant wife and seven children. The guide was a college graduate. I wondered how this was even possible, given her family circumstances. She described some of the horrendous conditions under which the miners worked. Kids as young as 10 or 11 worked in the mines. Women, who were considered unlucky underground, were forbidden to work there. They worked aboveground, however, separating the mineral-rich stones for processing. Many miners died of silicosis, and because it was perpetually damp, they suffered from respiratory illnesses. And then, of course, there were explosions.

Our charming and personable guide to the mine.

Rodrigo, looking brave, and Carmen, holding on for dear life, prepare to lead us into the mine.

We viewed many interesting photos from the mine's working days, then put on hard hats in what had been the miners' dressing room and proceeded to go underground! One of the most unsavory details was the *cuba*. It was the bucket that held human excrement (I didn't even want to know about the mule excrement!), and the man who carried it up got extra pay.

Our final hotel, a real gem, was in Mineral del Chico, in the heart of El Chico National Park, Mexico's first, which was established at about the same time as Yosemite in the States. Now the hotel is owned by a family, and one of the daughters told me of its history. First, it was a prison, then a casino, and then a hotel for the staff of wealthy people who stayed up the street at the Hotel Paradiso, owned by Pemex (the nationalized gas industry in Mexico). Her parents then bought it. They had and continue to have an extremely high standard for cleanliness and customer service. There were flowers from their own garden everywhere and turn-down service with chocolates on the pillow.

We met for drinks in an exquisite outside space in the hotel before having dinner in the hotel's dining room. Someone mentioned wanting to eat trout, a specialty of the area, and there was some disappointment that none was on the menu. Soon thereafter, a chef appeared. I assumed he was the chef of the restaurant in which we were eating, but in fact, he was the chef of a trout restaurant down the street called La Trucha Grilla (The Trout Grill). He proceeded to tell us of the 15 ways he prepared trout at his place, and we made a reservation for the following night. In your wildest dreams, can you imagine a restaurant in the U.S. allowing the chef of a competing place to come in and tout his wares? Only in Mexico. And how did he get there? Our waiter, overhearing our desire to eat trout, must have called him to come over.

Sunday morning, we breakfasted at 8 in the hotel dining room, and met Martin, who, along with his wife, Elena, would be hosting us for lunch at their home nearby. We headed out for about two and a half hours of bird-watching and hiking in the national park, which comprised nearly 7,000 acres. We were driven to the bottom of the road that entered the park. The area reminded me a lot of Pennsylvania's forests, except for one major difference: epiphytes (organisms that grow on the surface of plants and derive their moisture and nutrients from the air and rain).

After walking into the park for a while, Rodrigo mimicked the sounds of a diurnal owl and another bird of prey, both of which, he said, would get the attention of the birds in the area. It took a while, but after 10 to 15 minutes, we could hear two other owls responding, and we were surrounded by lots of different birds, which Rodrigo patiently pointed out and located in his scope for our viewing pleasure.

Rodrigo making the call of an owl, which had the desired results.

When we came to a *mirador* (lookout), we climbed up to see the view. This proved to be difficult, as the steps were not in the best condition, although I was thankful for the handrails, which are not always a guarantee in Mexico. By this time, it was intensely hot, and at over 9,000 feet, most of us were really feeling it. The views were definitely worth the exertion. We didn't stay long, as other tourists there were rowdy and clowning around in a dangerous manner. Rodrigo called Juanito on his cellphone, and the van lumbered up the road to pick us up. It was an extremely difficult ride back down the road on the other side, and we loudly applauded Juanito's driving skill when we were once again on a paved road.

Of all the highlights and treats on this trip, and there were many, the time spent at the home of Martin and Elena was the best. We went to their exquisite house and property for a gourmet lunch, *asti spumante*, *jamaica* (a nonalcoholic drink made from hibiscus flowers, which I adore), and homemade cheesecake for dessert. Before we dug in, Martin made a toast to all of us and welcomed us to their home. Overwhelmed by this hospitality, I started to cry, and individually Rodrigo, Carmen, Martin, and Elena all came over to comfort me.

A beautiful table had been set for all of us on the shaded back patio. Waiting to dig in is Juanito, our driver.

My (first) plateful.

After the meal, we just sat around talking. Martin brought out his guitar and sang some wonderful Mexican songs. I am embarrassed that I don't have a single picture of our hosts. When we first arrived, they were occupied getting everything out and everyone settled, and I was busy photographing their place, and then it just slipped my mind. We had a tour of their veggie gardens, their orchard, and the rest of the property.

As we boarded the van to return us to our hotel, we bid Martin and Elena a tearful adiós and got a last look at their home. While we drove away, others in the van thanked me for my expression of emotion before lunch because that's how they all were feeling.

Martin and Elena's huge, stunning home and property, the likes of which I had not seen before in Mexico.

The story of dinner at the trout restaurant is something to hear. When we first arrived, it was almost dusk, so the chef whisked us through one of the most disorganized back rooms I'd ever seen, outside to see his herb garden and fruit trees. We returned to the table to have an exquisite, nicely paced trout dinner. Martin and Elena made a surprise visit, stopping in for dinner with us on their way back to the city from their weekend retreat.

Our whole group enjoying dinner together at the trout restaurant.

After dinner, I noticed an unusual ring on Carmen's hand that hadn't been there earlier. Turns out it was made of a snail shell. Both Kevin and I wanted to buy ones like it, but the stall that sold them was closed for the night and we were making an early getaway the next morning before it reopened. Now it just so happened that the daughter of the chef and his wife worked at the ring place. A call was made to her and she appeared with about eight to 10 different rings like Carmen's for us to choose from, each for 60 pesos ($5.25 USD). Because she was a savvy salesperson, she also brought shawls, pillow covers, and purses (all hand-embroidered), in case we were interested in those, too.

As it was a cool night, we'd had a fire in the fireplace, and somebody mentioned marshmallows. Instantly, the five-year-old son of the chef appeared with a bag of marshmallows and sticks for all, putting them on the table and saying in perfect English, "Here they are." (His grandmother is an English teacher.) I believe that only in Mexico would this entire scenario have unfolded. This, and the afternoon at Martin and Elena's, is so emblematic of the friendliness, kindness, and hospitality of the Mexican people.

Monday morning, we had a quick breakfast and got on the road to return to San Miguel. But first, we spent about an hour walking around the local Lake Cedral, where many workers were busy cleaning up after the weekend campers, a few of whom were still in residence. It still looked like Pennsylvania to me…

After a long day of riding, about an hour outside of San Miguel, we stopped for *barbacoa*, a treat I'd never had before. While there were dozens of barbacoa places along a certain stretch of road, Rodrigo knew the best. It was gigantic but not at all crowded on a Monday afternoon. Barbacoa is not barbecue. It is young lamb, wrapped in agave leaves that impart a unique flavor, cooked overnight in a pot over hot stones in a pit dug into the ground. It is served with lime, sea salt, chopped onion, three kinds of salsa, and handmade blue corn and regular tortillas, of a little thicker variety than I was used to. Using whatever ingredients you liked—or in my case all of them—you constructed tacos for yourself. The lamb was arranged on a platter with the fatter cuts at one end, which I appreciated but didn't touch. The lovely leaner pieces were equally delicious. We arrived back in San Miguel at around 4 p.m.

Let me close with two interesting shots from the campgrounds.

This is the Mexican equivalent of American paint ball,
which you could do at this park.

And what was this truck doing in Mexico? It wasn't old, and no attempt had been
made to paint out the former owner.

Only in **SMA**

There is a Civil List in San Miguel where subscribers can ask questions, exchange information, put out an alarm, announce a lost dog, etc., to a large number of people quickly. Once, a person asked where she could purchase a cast-iron frying pan, and soon an answer came back, saying that Dr. XYZ, a veterinarian, sold them in his office. Then over the next few days, information was exchanged as to where his office was located and how to get there. On about day three, a posting came up asking, "I hate to be clueless here, but why would a veterinarian be selling cast-iron frying pans in his office?" One wag replied, "Because this is Mexico." He then went on to say that "…years earlier, this type of situation was much more common than today."

Mexicans look at death "...face to face, with impatience, disdain, or irony."

Octavio Paz

CHAPTER 2

2014

DÍA DE LOS MUERTOS (DAY OF THE DEAD) THROUGH THE YEARS

There are actually two days to celebrate Día de los Muertos: November 1st, to remember infants and children who have died, and the 2nd, to recall deceased adults. During this period it is believed that the veil between the living and the dead is at its thinnest and that the spirits of the dead come back to earth to be with their loved ones. Originating in central Mexico, Day of the Dead is an amalgamation of two religions, that of the Indigenous people of Mexico and the Catholicism of the conquering Spaniards. The Aztecs had the feast days of the Little Dead Ones and the Adult Dead. These death-related festivities coincided with the Catholic All Saints' Day and All Souls' Day, and so were incorporated into the Church holidays in the same way that early Christians incorporated Roman and other pagan holidays into their own religious celebrations.

But in 2014 in San Miguel de Allende, Day of the Dead festivities took place over four days. On October 30, Mujeres en Cambio, a non-profit organization on whose board I sit and for whom I do a lot of work, hosted its annual Day of the Dead tea, this year called Death by Chocolate. Tea sandwiches were offered, along with a selection of beverages, but the main event was the chocolate desserts.

The owner of Mente Cacao (Chocolate Mind, not Chocolate Mint, as you might think), an all-things-chocolate shop in town with several locations, brought displays of cocoa pods and beans, offered us a chocolate drink made with Kahlua, and gave us a short course on chocolate, opening with the reminder that chocolate was first a drink of the Aztecs. The chocolate bar, he said, has been around for only about 300 years.

On a magnificent afternoon, we sat in our hosts' huge garden to enjoy our treats and hear about the successes and needs of Mujeres en Cambio, which, through putting on monthly events such as this one, earns money to provide scholarships to girls from the *campo* (countryside) to attend high school and university. This year, we are supporting 165 girls.

A stunningly decked-out participant in the La Calaca parade.

That evening, there was a Catrina parade as part of La Calaca (a colloquial Mexican Spanish name for a skeleton) Festival. That event started about four blocks from my apartment and worked its way up Calle Hidalgo toward the jardín. By the sounds of the accompanying trumpets and tubas that were increasing in intensity, I knew they were near, so I dashed to the corner just in time to catch them going by, and then followed the musicians and costumed marchers to their destination.

A far more somber event awaited in the jardín: a demonstration of anger over the disappearance of 43 students from a teacher-training college in Ayotzinapa, in the state of Guerrero, in southwest Mexico, after a dispute with police. There were photos of all of the young men who are missing. Candles were lit, speeches were made, and banners of support were hung on the fence around *la parroquia* (enormous, stunning parish church, probably the most-photographed edifice in SMA, if not in all of Mexico). One banner said: "They took them alive; we want them back alive. We are all Ayotzinapa. San Miguel de Allende is with you." Other signs said "Mexico wounded" and "Mexico cries." Quite chilled, both physically and spiritually, I made my way back home through throngs of people and apparitions.

This might be a good time for a little history and explanation of Spanish terms used here that you might not know, gleaned from various of my readings.

"The Catrina was originally an engraving by José Guadalupe Posada (1852-1913)... Before being called Catrina, the image of a skeleton wearing a showy hat was called 'La Calavera Garbancera' and it was a representation of Indigenous Mexicans who were chickpea sellers and pretended to have European roots, and although they were poor, they wanted to show a lifestyle that they did not have. In the engraving the skeleton is nude because it is also a reference to the poverty that Mexicans were living in at that time.

"Muralist Diego Rivera took the image of the Calavera Garbancera and in his mural titled 'Dream of a dominical afternoon in the Alameda,' he painted the calavera and dressed it up with showy dresses and called her for the first time 'Catrina.' The image mocked the high class during the Porfiriato era (1876-1911)." (*Atención*, October 31, 2014)

"'Calaca' ... is a figure of a skull or skeleton (usually human) commonly used for decoration during the Mexican Day of the Dead festival. Calacas are frequently shown with marigold flowers.... They are often shown wearing festive clothing, dancing, and playing musical instruments to indicate a happy afterlife. This draws on the Mexican belief that no dead soul likes to be thought of sadly, and that death should be a joyous occasion. This goes back to Aztec beliefs, one of the few traditions to remain after the Spanish conquest." (Wikipedia) "The elaborate depictions of skeletons involved in everyday activities are never macabre but a reaffirmation of life and a triumphant snub against the inevitability of its passing." (*Atención*, October 31, 2014)

The original Catrina.

2014 was the second year of the La Calaca Festival in San Miguel, with many parties, loud music, and elements that some in the city feel are not fitting with the historic roots of the holiday. There are tensions around this.

The Aztecs believed that the pungent scent of marigolds helped the spirits of the deceased find their way back to earth, and marigolds rule the holiday. It is the only time of year that they are around. I like the color and aroma of the flower and bought some for my apartment.

Carlos, my Spanish teacher, warned me of a grave cultural error some gringos make, and that is to give a bouquet of marigolds to someone. This is tantamount to wishing them dead. There is the belief, also, that spirits come back as monarch butterflies to visit on this one special day of the year, and darned if I didn't see three butterflies in one block in the center of the city on this day.

The next day, Halloween, is a holiday the Mexicans don't generally celebrate. It has slowly become traditional in San Miguel for the gringos to give out candy to the Mexican children in costume in the jardín. I decided to buy something other than candy for the kids and had fun shopping for little gifts that I thought they might enjoy: balloons, barrettes, fake Mexican money, erasers, super balls, temporary tattoos.

Midday, I went to the *biblioteca* (library, the cultural and social center of the gringo community) on an errand and was enchanted by the decorations and altar there. "Altars are constructed all over town in memory of deceased loved ones or famous people, and all contain similar elements: a glass of water to quench the souls' thirst after their long journey; salt to purify the soul and to scare away the bad spirits; candles to help guide the souls' way to their homes; incense for cleaning the house of bad spirits and to protect the souls; flowers as a sign of festivity and to make the loved ones happy; palm straw to be used as the base of the offering and as a cushion where the soul can rest; sugar cane; and *pan de muertos*, bread in the shape of bones and dusted with sugar. The bread, an element added by Catholicism, represents Jesus' body. Optional elements include a picture of the honored person and his or her favorite foods." *(Atención*, October 31, 2014)

In the early evening, I attended a potluck costume party at the home of a friend. I wore my extremely cool glow-in-the-dark skeleton jacket that I had bought in Guanajuato during Cervantino. Its zipper goes all the way to the top of the head, bringing together a skull with

I got into the spirit of Día de los Muertos in my special skeleton jacket.

only the eyes cut out. I find it quite humorous that my glasses protrude from the eyeholes. Because they were the only openings when I bought it, I had to get my seamstress to open up the mouth, also, as my glasses got steamed up when I breathed if it was cold.

One little girl with a foot in both cultures (with calaca makeup and plastic pumpkin Halloween treat collector) waits patiently for some goodies.

After we ate and drank, prizes were awarded for the best costumes. Then we were off to the jardín en masse. On the way there, we came across a street party being hosted by Vía Orgánica, an organic food market and restaurant. As we neared the jardín, I peeled off, went home to get my trick-or-treat goodies for the kids, and put on my heavy coat over my skeleton jacket; it was that cold and windy. When I started giving out the little gifts, I was almost instantly overwhelmed by what seemed like hundreds of children, all asking for their *"calaverita"* (little skeleton, sort of like saying "trick or treat"). I gave out 65 little trinkets in probably 65 seconds. I had my camera with me, but there was no time to ask anyone to take my picture. The kids loved the non-sweet treats, as friends had promised they would when I expressed doubt. Then I just walked around with my camera, enjoying the people and the atmosphere.

Many were out in enormously fabulous costumes for Halloween.

On Saturday, November 1, I went up to the jardín to view the altars put together by local schoolchildren and civil organizations under the direction of the Education and Culture Department of the city. One of the altars was especially meaningful to me, as I had known the deceased. He was Tambula, the newspaper seller in the jardín from whom I bought my *Atención* newspaper every Friday. His basso profundo voice reverberated there when he called out the names of the papers he carried.

The main offering was a tribute to Tehua, "the best voice of Mexican folkloric music," who lived in SMA for 20 years before going to Mexico City to advance her career. Tehua was an aunt to Claudia, the wife of my Spanish teacher. Respected and beloved by old sanmiguel-enses, Tehua succumbed to cancer in August 2014. Recordings of her singing played in a loop.

These elegant catrinas bookended one of the displays.

Even the pooches in town get into the act, this one with her
Day of the Dead jacket. Could she be any cuter?

When these friendly and handsome flower salesmen saw me taking a photo
of them and their wheelbarrow, they posed for me.

Skilled face painters were doing a brisk business.

I wore a lovely outfit of black and silver, but it was so (uncharacteristically) cold that I had to wear a shawl over it all. I was happy to have my reversible (silver/gold) sombrero de bruja *(witch's hat) to wear.*

As the afternoon sun's rays lengthened, preparations began for that evening. Saturday night was the eagerly awaited annual art walk and altar viewing at Fábrica la Aurora, a former textile mill now repurposed as artist studios and showrooms, and the place to see and be seen.

On Sunday, November 2, the main Day of the Dead, I did what I have traditionally done for three years now. I went with friends for

This skeletal musician joined others at the Fábrica in a tableau of a group of workers from the past who played in a band together in their off-hours.

These partygoers in elaborate costumes and makeup are representative of hundreds of others out for the evening at this annual blow-out event.

brunch at Los Bisquets restaurant, and then we joined with thousands of others to go to the nearby cemetery, buying flowers along the way to place on the gringo graves, which are rather sad and plain compared to those on the Mexican side. I decided not to take any photos this year, as I have taken so many over the years, and it feels disrespectful to me.

"At the heart of the festival with all of its wonderful costumes, revelry, art, and tales was a celebration of life, and the embracing of our very real mortality. Young and old came together and perhaps grew a bit more courageous about how they live their lives, and the memories they are creating." (Geoff Livingston, *Atención*, November 7, 2014)

2015

THE MERCADO DE ALFEÑIQUES AT PLAZA CIVICA, OCTOBER 31

Every year, in the same spot, Plaza Civica, dozens of vendors of *alfeñiques* set up shop to provide components for the altars to deceased loved ones that virtually everyone creates in their homes, offices, stores, or public spaces. Alfeñiques are folk art objects made from sugar paste, which originated in Italy, but which were brought to Mexico from Spain along with Catholicism by the conquistadores, where they became part

One of the many stalls offering alfeñiques.

of Day of the Dead starting around the 17th or 18th century. Alfeñiques (the word comes from Arabic) replaced the Aztec tradition of making figurines for altars out of amaranth. One of the main production centers for the alfeñiques figures is in Guanajuato, the state in which San Miguel is located. Of course, lots of other altar essentials, home decorations, and costume elements are also sold at these temporary booths.

BACK TO THE JARDÍN, OCTOBER 31

The jardín was looking especially festive, planted with *cempasuchil (flor de muertos)*—marigolds. As the day progressed, so did the demand for face painting. I saw more face painters this year than ever before. Lines formed behind each artist. At 100 pesos (about $6 USD) a clip, these enterprising folks were making some serious money this weekend.

All ages got their turn with the face painters.

Burros carrying thrilled or apprehensive children went round and round.

Food vendors were having a very good day. This one is selling homemade ice cream.

What would any fiesta day in the jardín be without a mojiganga, *a huge* papel-mâché *puppet?*

Kids behind bars; I found this sight of children seemingly imprisoned in Starbucks particularly compelling.

I couldn't resist taking a photo of this lovely lady with her three chihuahuas, all dressed up for the occasion. I met her again that evening in yet other outfits for herself and the dogs.

And as if there wasn't quite enough going on in town that evening, a bullfight was scheduled (yes, SMA has its own bullring), a somewhat rare event these days. However, I did not make an appearance or even consider doing so. You'll recall my family's first—and last—attendance at a bullfight from the prologue of *A Lifetime to Get Here: San Miguel de Allende:* "Besides visiting archeological sites such as Monte Alban, we went to a bullfight. Our driver took us there early and we watched the preliminaries with much anticipation. However, when the actual bullfight began, we were horrified and fled back to the car."

Taking in the La Calaca Festival
in Parque Juarez, October 31

The La Calaca Festival is now in its third year, and its mission is to keep alive the practices of Day of the Dead in San Miguel. Each year it sponsors new and different events to that end. As I made my way to the park to see one of them, I admired many of the *tiendas* (stores) that were decorated for the holiday with marigolds.

I couldn't let this sight go undocumented. Even the flower seller can afford a cellphone. Well, hooray for that!

Then it was on to the pièce de résistance of La Calaca Festival, and my main reason for coming to the park: *El Pirámide de Muertos* (The Pyramid of the Dead Ones), situated just next to a basketball court. (This type of juxtaposition here no longer surprises me.) It was actually quite tall, and still a work in progress. It featured framed *homenajes* (homages)

The Pyramid of the Dead Ones.

A breathtakingly beautiful view up Calle Aldama that I caught on my way home.

to the recently and not-so-recently deceased. Some assemblages were light-hearted. Others were to promote causes, like Colectiva 41, a drop-in center for LGBT youth.

At dusk, I donned my skeleton jacket once again and took my bag of non-candy treats to the jardín to give to the costumed children who have now embraced Halloween, much to the distress of many Mexicans.

Some folks go all out with their costuming.

ART WALK AND ALTAR VIEWING
AT FÁBRICA LA AURORA, OCTOBER 31

Every year for Day of the Dead, Fábrica la Aurora invites the public in for drinks and snacks—and, hopefully, shopping. The artists put up their own personal altars, and it draws huge crowds of costumed lookers. The first thing visitors see when they enter is a colossal altar, done each year by the same man, a former textile worker, I believe, which lifts up some aspect of the long-ago mill workers' lives.

Then I joined the throngs walking around and gawking at the art, the altars, and some pretty-outlandishly dressed characters. What fun!

A catrina taking a rest after visiting all of the altars, perhaps?

I spotted a large, elaborate altar as I was exiting the Fábrica, constructed to honor the 50th anniversary of the 24-Hour Association, a membership group that is legally able to act as the next-of-kin of a deceased foreigner, dealing with the remains, following the deceased's previously indicated wishes as to burial, cremation, etc., and securing death certificates, a notoriously difficult document to get in a timely fashion.

The long list of the names at the altar is only those whom the organization has served in 2015. I knew several of the people on that list. I am a member of this organization, which spares grieving family members, who may not even have a passport, the agony of getting to San Miguel and dealing with the government around the demise of their loved one within 24 hours of the death, as bodies here must be either in the ground or cremated within that time period, thus the name of the organization.

VIEWING MORE SPECIALTY ALTARS, NOVEMBER 1

The annual Service of Remembrance of Departed Loved Ones took place at the Unitarian Universalist Fellowship of San Miguel de Allende (UUFSMA) on November 1. It always includes an altar containing the requisite items, to which attendees are invited to add photos of their deceased friends and family members.

I never miss an opportunity to stop by the altar in the courtyard of the fabulous store Camino Silvestre (the Wild Way), owned by Jim and Alfredo, friends of my daughter and son-in-law. Their store is centered on birds and butterflies, and each year they outdo themselves with their altar dedicated to endangered species. This year, hundreds of folded paper *colibríes* (hummingbirds) are hanging by filament from the ceiling as part of the altar.

A stunning altar painstakingly and lovingly erected each year by bird-centric store Camino Silvestre, this year honoring hummingbirds.

That evening, solemnity and merriment existed side-by-side in the jardín. As darkness fell, students lit hundreds of candles as part of their public altars. And the parroquia served as backdrop to a stage for a catrina parade and musical entertainment, and *papel picado* (cut paper) fluttered above it all.

Papel picado flapping in the breeze.

VISIT TO ONE OF THE LOCAL CEMETERIES ON DAY OF THE DEAD, NOVEMBER 2

I repeated my much-loved custom of going with a friend for breakfast at a restaurant very close to the cemetery, then buying flowers as we walked with throngs of others to the graveyard. We headed right for the gringo side to place our flowers on some of the graves of the *extranjeros* (foreigners) who have gone before us, some of whom I knew.

All of the time we were at the cemetery, we could hear the amplified voice of a priest conducting Mass and the occasional strains of a mariachi band hired by a family for the occasion.

We met friends, stopped to talk, shed a few tears, used up all of our flowers, and then headed over to the Mexican side for a very different experience. Restraint is not a word one would use for what is encountered there.

This beautifully decorated gravesite is that of Toller Cranston, former Canadian Olympic medalist figure skater who revolutionized the form, and more recently painter, interior decorator, writer, illustrator, costume designer, choreographer, and bon vivant. He died in SMA in January 2015 at age 65.

One of the last of the catrinas until next year's Día de los Muertos.

2016

In late October, when I went to my usual Saturday breakfast with friends at Mama Mia, I noticed the profusion of marigolds and red wine-colored cockscomb, the traditional flowers of the holiday, which had seemingly sprung up overnight, decorating buildings, shop windows, church gardens, and more.

*I ran into a fellow student from my Spanish class
and insisted on taking her picture.*

The night of Saturday, October 29, was one of the biggest bashes this burg sees in any year. It is the annual altar-viewing party at Fábrica la Aurora, a former huge textile mill repurposed as artists' studios and galleries. Everyone was dressed to the nines and/or as catríns and ca-trinas. Each gallery displayed its own altar and all were decorated with marigolds. Most offered drinks and some, snacks. Musicians played in many spots. Of course, the artists' work was for sale, too.

I attended the party clad in this ensemble:

🌿 a 75-peso (less than $4 USD) veiled hat with flower, bought
that day at the alfeñiques market;

❦ a heavy black Mexican-style skirt, bought in Philly;

❦ a thrift-shop black blouse, bought with my sister Gretchen
  in Chester County, Pennsylvania, last summer;

❦ a black burned-velvet jacket, bought at a used-clothing
  store in SMA;

❦ hidden black tights;

❦ an evening bag and necklace from Morocco;

❦ and skull earrings from the Hippie Market at Cervantino
  in Guanajuato several years ago.

It takes a world, it seems, to dress me.

I love dressing up for this fiesta each year.

Then I spent the next couple of hours meeting friends and taking their photos and those of strangers whose outfits intrigued me, and admiring all of the altars and magnificent gallery displays.

This altar blew me away with its skulls covered in minuscule beads.
The amount of work required to make something like this boggles my mind!

Here I am with two dear friends, Jorge and Alejandro. I am laughing because
Alejandro's hat is pushing mine off my head.

My friend Paula, usually a winter-only resident of SMA, came down from Maryland for a week to experience Day of the Dead for the first time.

These ladies, with the most extravagant of hats, told me they'd bought them at the newly opened Museum of the Catrina. I'm not sure whether it will remain open year-round or if it is just for the season of Day of the Dead.

On our way out, we passed músicos *playing, and watched as this very talented couple danced the tango elegantly.*

The following day, I attended the service at my Unitarian Universalist congregation, as I always do on a Sunday. We had our own altar where members and friends could place photos of loved ones, and a part of the service was dedicated to remembrance of those who had died in the past year. Rev. Wyman Rousseau, a retired UU minister now living in SMA with his wife, gave an excellent sermon on "The Burden and Blessing of Mortality."

On Monday, Halloween day, we had Spanish class as usual, and, also as usual, our maestra, Alejandra, had fun prepared for us. We learned a new meaning for the word calaveritas—the same word used earlier by trick-or-treating youngsters for "little skeletons." In this new-to-us context, the word means irreverent, often-ridiculous poems, written as an epitaph in traditional Mexican verse (rhyming), portraying people as if they were already dead (wishful thinking?). They are used to channel feelings that in any other context would be difficult to express, and are usually accompanied by drawings of skulls. They first appeared in the late 19th century, and the ones about unpopular politicians were often censored or destroyed. Alejandra presented us with two examples she found on the Internet, one about Mexico's current president, Peña-Nieto, and the other about the Republican candidate for U.S. president, both poems very clever and funny. Then we each picked the name of another classmate out of a hat, and wrote—in rhyming Spanish, quite the challenge!—a calaverita for that person. After corrections, we wrote them on good paper, read them to each other, and presented them to the "honorees." Alejandra gave us little paper skull stickers and markers to decorate them, after which we all went outside to our class's altar to hang them up.

Alejandra then produced a large loaf of pan de muertos—the light, vaguely sweet bread with the shape of bones on top that I'd read about in *Atención* (it's baked only around Day of the Dead)—and a container of *nata*, the cream at the top of a bottle of unhomogenized milk, to spread on the slices she cut and distributed. Yum!

All the next day, hundreds of sanmiguelenses worked very hard creating altars from natural products (beans, rice, chiles, etc.) and pan de muertos, alfeñiques, and other remembrances of the departed; these circled the jardín. That night, it rained hard for hours. My heart sank. The creations would be ruined. The next day, Day of the Dead itself, I went up to see them, and while they weren't exactly ruined, they were sad, dispirited reminders of their former selves. Flowing water had cut gullies into the natural materials that had been laid out on the ground to create pictures. The papel picado hung limp and pale, as much of the color had leached out.

This year, I didn't follow my usual practice of having breakfast at a restaurant near the cemetery, buying flowers at one of the stalls along the route there, and then visiting the graves and niches of those people I've known who have died here, a number that grows every year, of course. Instead, I had yoga first, then a massage, then lunch, and got off around 2 p.m. to begin my mission. It was very hot and crowded, but I made my rounds, and saw the gravesites of two friends from my UU congregation who had passed in 2016 and others from previous years. I placed marigolds and cockscomb on many of the graves of people I did not know on the gringo side, and then rested in the shade before leaving. I saw one discordant note that has really stayed with me. Two very young women were keeping vigil at a gravesite. They had pushed large candles into the dirt near the gravestone, and lit them. And there they sat, heads bowed... texting on their cellphones. Somehow, they missed the message of the day. How very sad.

"Instructions for life: Pay attention. Be astonished. Tell about it."

Mary Oliver

CHAPTER 3

2016

MUCH TIME HAS PASSED...

This marks my eighth year in San Miguel, and while I'm neither jaded nor disinterested in what's going on, I have attended most of the major annual events many times and the pop-up events as they have occurred; I have blogged about and photographed them extensively. I am now well into my 70s and have slowed down some and made a few accommodations to that new reality. For example, instead of schlepping a bottle of wine a week from La Europea, I order wine by the case from there, which has the side benefit of triggering a 10 percent discount; an additional discount when I pay cash, which I always do; and free delivery to my apartment. I pay a student to make Costco runs for me (along with many other customers in the same trip). She brings me multiples of heavy items such as almond milk, big bags of granola, and frozen blueberries. I also sometimes take the bus to my destination when I am sure that I have already walked my 10,000 steps for the day.

In this year, also, I am working hard on preparing for publication, with the help of an editor and a designer, my first book, *An Orchid Sari: The Personal Diary of an American Mom in 1960s India*, so that I do not have as much time available as almost-daily blogs require. What I have done instead is to chronicle the many things that happen to me from just living my life here and that certainly seem worth writing about. So, from this point on, I will be writing short pieces in an as-they-occurred format with many fewer photos.

SOMETIME IN FEBRUARY

A SMALL MIRACLE

My friend Ann and I attended the movie *Boyhood* one afternoon at the Pocket Theater, and on the way out, we saw a bunch of wadded-up pesos that someone had dropped on the stone stairs leading up to the street. I whisked them up and we decided not to ask the 12 to 15 people there if they'd dropped any money, as all would have probably said yes. I stuck the bills into my pocket and said we could put it toward buying our dinner. At that quick glance, I saw 170 pesos (around $9 USD), but there may have been more. Not five steps away from the theater, we saw a very old, nearly-bent-in-half beggar woman, and I instantly took out the found loot and thrust it into her outstretched hand. Ann and I both felt so good! The old woman must have thought she'd died and gone to heaven. What are the chances that she would be there begging right after we found the money? (I've never seen a beggar anywhere on that block before or since as the sidewalk is so narrow.)

I make it a practice not to give money to beggars, as there was a front-page article in *Atención* asking us not to, explaining that it ties people to the streets and that there are a myriad of programs at DIF (Desarrollo Integral de la Familia, a Mexican public institution of social assistance that focuses on strengthening and developing the welfare of the Mexican family) to help them; they do not need to resort to begging. But on this afternoon, it seemed the right thing to do under the circumstances, and I don't regret it.

MID-APRIL

UN VIAJE PARA VER UN ARBOL
(A TRIP TO SEE A TREE)

I didn't go to see just any tree, of course, but one of the finest examples of Mexico's national tree, the Montezuma bald cypress, *sabino* in Spanish, *ahuehuete* (old man of the water) in Nahuatl.

Two friends of mine—Susan and her daughter Kirsten—invited anyone in our Saturday morning breakfast group who wanted to see the famous 500-year-old sabino tree in the nearby village of La Huerta (the truck farm, the garden, or the orchard) to join them after breakfast the following Saturday. I bit and was the only one.

I responded to Susan's email by asking if I needed to wear more sturdy shoes than my strappy sandals and if I needed to pack a lunch, and telling her that I had to be back in SMA for a 5:30 dinner date with my friend Phyllis. She replied that my sandals were fine and that we'd be back in plenty of time for lunch, not to mention dinner. Famous last words!

On Saturday, we made our way at around 11 a.m. to the bus station behind the San Juan de Dios Market. A bus schedule hung on a wall, with times filled in with chalk. The name of the town we were headed for was not there, but Susan recognized the name La Presa (the dam, which she knew we had to cross) on one of the buses, and I (as the best Spanish-speaker of us three) asked the driver if it were going to La Huerta and, if so, at what time. Evidently, we had just missed a bus going to that destination, because the next one wasn't due for 50 more minutes. Since it was a hot day, I suggested that we sit on the benches in the shade rather than in the bus to wait. However, Susan noticed that the bus was rapidly filling and thought maybe we'd better get on it if we were going to have a seat. Good call! The bus became more and more crowded with mostly women and children and huge plastic bags of their purchases. Since every little town has a couple of tiendas, these folks were probably stocking up on goods from the "big city" to sell in their local stores or perhaps for their very large families.

The bus departed on time with many passengers standing. Happily, Susan had gone on this trip before—10 years ago—and so more or less knew the route and could tell that we were headed in the right direction. However, after more than an hour passed and lots of stops were made and many people got off, I got a bit nervous and would ask at each one, "*¿Es La Huerta?*" ("Is this La Huerta?") and all would be answered with, "*No, más allá.*" ("No, farther on.") Finally, after an hour and half on the road, the bus pulled into a village and turned around to go back the other way, and we spotted a sign that said "*Arbol Sabino*" with an arrow pointing to the object of our trip. We were there at last! Before we stepped off the bus, I asked the driver what time the next bus came. I thought he said 3:15, but he might have said 3:40. It was now about 1:15.

Finally! What we'd come to see!

We followed the arrow, climbed some steep stairs, and saw the tree! We were not disappointed! It was humongous and in perfect condition.

A sign nearby gave us some valuable information, including that it takes 18 to 20 people holding outstretched arms to encircle the trunk. It said that this species takes a long time to grow and is a relative of the California sequoia. The oldest sabino in the world is at Santa Maria de Tule in Oaxaca, Mexico, with an age of approximately 2,000 years. The sabino grows only in places with abundant water. In the case of this specimen, it has reached such a great size thanks to the spring that nurtures it.

Susan and I are dwarfed by this magnificent specimen.

Although the village's name suggests a farm, garden, or orchard, none of those was in sight—and I wasn't really surprised. In fact, the village was incredibly dry, as was all of the land we had driven through, and indeed as it is in San Miguel de Allende, our departure point.

We spent about 15 minutes walking around the tree and taking photos. That was it. Party over. Tree seen and admired. We learned a few things. Now what?

We decided that our next goal was to find something to eat and drink, which turned out to be easier said than done, but we finally located a tienda, which was pretty well stocked. I had probably one of the best canned sodas I've ever drunk. It was fresh pineapple juice with mineral water—so cool and refreshing. I also bought a small bag of homemade popcorn, which was neither oversalted nor buttered, just the way I like it. Susan had juice and a pastry, and Kirsten some chips and a drink.

We found a lowish stone wall, made ourselves as comfortable as we could on the flatter stones, and proceeded to eat our "lunch" and also to provide entertainment for some of the locals. I said *"Buenas tardes"* ("Good afternoon") to everyone, either on foot or in a car or truck, as I knew that Mexicans perceived silence as rudeness. One toothless elderly lady engaged us in conversation, asking if we had come to see the tree. Well…yes. Why else in the world would we be there?

After eating, we moved back to the "bus stop" and sat on yet another stone wall to wait.

We passed some time reading the remnants of this sign, which said that in 2009, there were 266 inhabitants in La Huerta.

If anyone ever tells you that nothing goes on in a small town, do not believe it for one second. First, we took in the passing parade. A bunch of boys perhaps 10 to 12 years old appeared with a darling puppy and a lasso. They were, of course, lassoing the puppy, which caused us great upset, and then each other, much less. Because of the heat and the weight of my backpack, I had removed it and put it on the wall, a bit away from me. I hated myself for doing so, but when I saw the boys I immediately put it back on. To assuage my guilt, I gave them the two-thirds-full bag of popcorn to finish off among them. They asked us lots of questions. It was clear that they had had some instruction in English. One asked in Spanish, "*Como se dice 'dame' en inglés?*" ("How do you say 'give me' in English?") When I replied, "Give me," that was followed by "Give me your money." Of course, they were smiling and we were smiling, so it was all in good fun, but I didn't feel quite so bad about reconnecting with my backpack.

They left and three bulls meandered down the road. They were spectacular-looking, in differing patterns of black and white. Unfortunately, my camera wasn't at the ready and I missed taking their photo.

A woman arrived with a large empty bucket and proceeded to a faucet to fill it. It was then that I surmised that the spring that feeds the sabino is also used by the residents of the pueblo, and that they have no running water! She walked away with the bucket on her head, held in place with one hand while the other was jauntily placed on her hip.

Nearby was a large and deep metal cooking pot filled with hot oil, where a woman was cooking *carnitas* (small pieces of pork) over an open fire. Many thin and scruffy dogs were milling around, brought close by the aroma. The woman kept kicking in their direction to make them move on. I was afraid that one would put its paws on the edge of the pot and turn the whole thing over onto itself. Happily, this did not occur. Customers came and went.

At 3:10, a young mother and her child arrived to wait for the bus. Hope leaped in our hearts, as surely this meant that the bus was coming at 3:15. Wrong. So then we waited none too patiently until 3:40. Still no bus, so I asked the woman what time the bus came, and she said, "*A las cuatro*" ("At four"). If she knew that the bus was coming at 4, why did she appear at 3:10? To look at us?

At 3:50, we could see the approaching bus, and rejoiced. But the driver had to have a carnitas torta before he prepared to drive off precisely at 4. We finally boarded. However, a car had appeared in the road where he needed to go, and he angrily waved the driver onto a side street. This stand-off lasted a few minutes, and finally the car's driver backed up instead of going forward as he had been asked to do. The car hit something, we heard the crash, and then all the water came out of his radiator. I had visions of the car's driver blaming the bus driver—and us having to sit there while they worked it out—but luckily that didn't happen.

But we were still not home free. A huge Pepsi delivery truck had parked by the side of the road, and there was no way the bus could pass the truck safely. The truck driver was nowhere to be seen. Much honking ensued. Eventually the truck driver returned (I think he was in the tienda where we had bought our drinks and snacks) and made more room for the bus on the road, and we were on our way. We made many stops, mostly for well-dressed men who I assumed were going into San Miguel for some Saturday night festivities.

We had passed through a long, unlighted tunnel on our way to La Huerta, and of course we had to re-enter it on the way back. It had only one lane. I don't even want to think about what happens when cars—or buses or trucks!—enter it from both directions at once. In the pitch dark, since there were no lights in the bus either, we suddenly heard a loud, smacking sound, and I felt liquid spray onto my ankles. Evidently a water bottle had fallen off the luggage rack above the seats, landed hard on the floor, and opened up, spraying everyone nearby.

The adventure was not yet over! About an hour later, we pulled up at Mega, a supermarket at the outskirts of town, and I dashed off the bus to catch a taxi, as I knew that some were always there. I was alone, waiting, when a man my age came out with a shopping cart full of groceries. He got next to me, but not behind me, and I made sure he knew that I was taking the next taxi. At that moment, three things happened almost simultaneously. A taxi arrived, the driver jumped out and opened his trunk, and a Mega worker appeared out of nowhere and began enthusiastically unloading the contents of the man's cart into the trunk. I sputtered and fumed, but very quickly realized that she was going to make a tip from the man and not from me, so I said *"Está bien"* ("It's OK") and walked away to another waiting taxi.

I arrived home with mere minutes to spare before my dinner date. I took off all my very dusty clothes, had a quick wash, including my sandals and feet, re-dressed, and met Phyllis stepping out of a taxi when I exited the courtyard of my building.

¡Viva México!

AUGUST 1

ASKING FOR HELP

I returned to my rented apartment in a condo development on Calle Mesones in El Centro as I always do on this date, following three months in Philadelphia. The condos are directly across from The Mint nightclub, where for years I had seen a phalanx of bouncers outside. Had I arrived before 6 p.m. on a weekday or before noon on a Saturday, the faithful *mozo* (there seems to be no end to how this word translates into English, but the mozo at my complex was a combination doorman, general cleaner and maintenance person, problem-solver and all-around helper—and super nice person) would have gladly carried my suitcases up to my third-floor apartment. And usually, after hours, the shuttle driver would help me with them, but this was a Saturday night probably around 10:30 p.m., Mesones was jumping, and The Mint was just getting started for the night. There was no place to park, so the driver just idled the van and carried my luggage into the courtyard.

I stood perplexed, trying to decide what to do. I could have taken it up piecemeal in plastic bags, but the thought of several trips to and from the third-floor apartment carrying heavy bags—after an all-day trip starting at the crack of dawn from Philadelphia on two planes and a shuttle—was far from appealing. Then I remembered the bouncers! I left my bags in the courtyard, screwed up my courage, crossed Mesones, and walked up to the oldest bouncer, hoping he was the boss. In my far-less-than-perfect Spanish, I explained my problem. Several of the younger men snickered, but the older man took me seriously, said a few words to the younger ones, and accompanied me across the street. In only one trip to the third floor, he carried all my suitcases in an admirable display of machismo. I thanked him profusely and tipped him lavishly, then closed the door behind me and collapsed on the sofa, thrilled with my success. I was imagining that when he showed the younger men the tip I had given him for less than five minutes of work, their snickering quickly ceased.

A few minutes later, the doorbell rang, and it was Juan, the bouncer cum bellhop, asking if he could give me his phone number so that if I had other jobs, I could call him. I took Juan's cell number but never needed his services again.

The Last Day of October

What a Storm! Global Climate Change at Work in San Miguel de Allende

A huge, violent rain, hail, and windstorm in SMA in late October never, ever happens—until yesterday!

In midafternoon, I left my apartment with posters advertising a Mujeres en Cambio event, with the plan of delivering them to five places of business in Centro. When I left, the weather was beautiful with a few nonthreatening clouds. But by the time I got to the third place, the Bagel Cafe, it was looking dire. I was going to pop into its bathroom to take off the turtleneck I was wearing under another shirt, as I was sweating bullets in the hot afternoon sun (the turtleneck had been a definite requirement in the morning), but I didn't, and am I glad! By the time I hung up the poster and proceeded to the front door, all hell had broken loose: The rain was coming down in buckets. Now occasionally this does happen in the late afternoon during the rainy season and lasts, oh, maybe 10 to 15 minutes; the sun then reappears and all activity resumes. But yesterday was different. Although the rainy season was supposedly over, it rained as I've never seen before—and it didn't stop.

So I took a seat on the cold cement steps in the entryway to the cafe to await the conclusion of the storm; two other people were waiting, also. Since I had nothing to do, I deleted some photos from my camera and then decided to photograph the storm, as by this time, Calle Correo, on which I was marooned, was running like a river.

Water, water everywhere!

Pretty soon, I was feeling drops from the window way above my head. I moved. And I watched. And I photographed. About this time, I could feel that the temperature had dropped considerably, probably at least 10 degrees, maybe more, and in my slightly sweaty turtleneck, I was now feeling chilled. Then it started to hail!

It does hail here from time to time, but it lasts only a few minutes. This hail went on for 15 minutes! The noise on the skylight above my head was deafening and I was afraid the weight of the rain and the steadily building hail might break the glass, so I moved again. Every time a car came by on Correo, it sprayed water up into the entryway where we were waiting. The cafe was trying to close, as it's open only for breakfast and lunch, but the two brothers who own it had an ad-

The owners/brothers madly mopping up.

Plastic trash bags were innovatively turned into raincoats.

Perhaps these are tourists wondering how to cross the street.

ditional task before they could lock up. Water was now coming over the second-floor balcony down to where I was standing, and water was cascading down the steps from the outer part of the restaurant that is open to the sky. Within the entryway was an additional door next to the restaurant's door, and water was coming out from underneath it, too.

*One of the signs I created on my computer and printed out
for the demonstration that didn't happen.*

Finally, after an hour and a half, it stopped raining. But the difficulty wasn't over yet, as all of the streets were rushing with water and crossing was difficult and dangerous.

I did finally get home, but by then I was very damp and cold. I wrote a quick email to the teacher of the English Chat at UNAM that I would not be appearing, as crossing the flooded streets was just a bit too much for me. We were to have had a vigil of ex-pats that night to demonstrate in opposition to the hatred, xenophobia, and racism coming out of the U.S. election. It was also Halloween night, when hundreds of parents bring their youngsters in costume to the jardín to receive candy and other treats from the gringos, and there are lots of other folks in costume and in a festive mood. It was the perfect night for it, but at 7 p.m., the hour that was called for it, there was still lightning in the sky (I could easily see it from my third-floor windows) and I was reluctant to go out. I was deeply, deeply disappointed, as I had my signs ready and wanted to communicate to our Mexican hosts how much I was against the foul rhetoric coming from my country. I don't think that the event came off, and I'm so hoping it will be rescheduled.

EARLY NOVEMBER

BAT IN THE BEDROOM!

Just as I was drifting off to sleep one night, I was jolted awake by the sound of what seemed to be very large wings beating. It sounded as if they were at the window, so I concluded they must be outside. I turned on the light, and the noise immediately stopped. I figured it wasn't a bird, and my mind clamped on the idea of a bat, because I am on the third and top floor of my complex, probably very near to where the bats hang out, if there are any. I got my flashlight and looked all around but couldn't spot anything. I tried to go back to sleep, but the beating began again. At that point, I shut the bedroom door and slept in the guest room.

The next morning when I opened the heavy drapes over my bedroom windows, I saw a shape hanging from the curtain cord between the window and the sheers. I pulled back the curtain, and it looked very much like a bat to me. Happily for me, it was asleep. When my housekeeper, Reyna, arrived, I showed her the "bat," and after some study, she told me that it was not a bat at all, but a gigantic *mariposa nocturna* (nocturnal butterfly—black in color). I was so relieved, as I truly detest bats. Reyna told me that mariposas nocturnas are considered a symbol of death in Mexico, which I, of course, dismissed. She wanted to hit it with a broom, but I insisted that she not kill it, but somehow get it to go outside while I was at yoga. I met her at the door to the complex as I was returning, and she assured me that that had been accomplished. Whew!

ONLY IN SAN MIGUEL

It's 12:30 p.m., and I am in a tienda that refills printer cartridges. I say to the clerk, all in Spanish:

"Good afternoon. I would like to exchange this empty cartridge for a new one."

"I'm sorry, Señora, but we don't have any filled ones at present, but we could fill this one for you in 40 minutes."

"OK, that's fine."

"It will be ready at 3 p.m."

"But aren't you closed between 2 and 4?"

"Yes, Señora, that is correct."

"So then, I should come after 4?"

"Yes."

"Are you sure it will be ready then? Should I call first to see if it is ready?"

"No, it will be ready."

Miracle of miracles, it was ready!

"We don't see things as they are, we see them as we are."

Anaïs Nin

CHAPTER 4

2017

NEW DIGS AND THAT'S JUST THE START OF IT

If my 2017 had a theme, it might be "newness." Every year has its new elements, of course. But by now, I felt that I had described many of my observations of life in SMA, so it seems natural that I would take special note of the new.

Absolutely the most dramatic change for me was making substantial progress in my goal of moving to a dream apartment. As the process began taking a different path from what I had envisioned, I had no idea of the quirks I would face along the way, including a space heater that had me doubting my intelligence for a bit and a newly privatized city trash system that made me think way too much about my garbage. The stories in this chapter tell about those events and more, and all have newness in common.

...YOU GET WHAT YOU NEED

From the time, perhaps eight years ago, when I first visited someone who lived in a Quinta Loreto casita, I lusted after one of the small homes. I, too, wanted to reside in a centrally located leafy compound with its own restaurant and swimming pool and friendly, helpful neighbors. But my hostess from that first visit warned me that I would have to wait for someone to die before a place became available, as no one ever voluntarily gave up their unit. Sometime later, after I was a dinner guest in one of the apartments there, I added one of those to my wish list as a close-second choice. After an extended time of longing, I visited Georgina at the Quinta Loreto office to inquire of the possibility of getting on the waiting list that I had been told existed for either type of housing.

With my desire to live there officially noted, I began a long wait. During that time, I learned many things about life at La Quinta, some good, some not so good. While the rents were incredibly cheap, and subletting was permitted during absences from places rented annually, tenants were responsible for the majority of changes and/or improvements they wanted in their units. One friend had to put a new roof on her three-bedroom casita. It fell to renters to order fill-ups for their outside gas tanks, and often the truck didn't arrive in a timely manner, or sometimes the driver cheated the customer. Water by the *garrafón* (five-gallon water container) had to be ordered, and much waiting around for a delivery was sometimes necessary. Tenants had to pay for electricity and Internet, also; besides the monthly bill, they were responsible for the original service set-up and pausing during times away. Errors in bills from the electric company were rampant and sometimes of frightening proportions.

The most daunting part to me was the thought of having to hire and pay a housekeeper, oversee her work, figure out the annual required *aguinaldo* (Christmas bonus, based on a complicated formula), and perhaps even have to let that person go for a myriad of possible reasons; a severance payment is required by law in that case. I had always rented from an owner who took on all of those responsibilities.

During the two interminable years that I cooled my heels waiting for an available place to rent, I came to the understanding—which infuriated me—that the waiting list had little bearing on who got into the next-available vacancy. Those already ensconced at Quinta Loreto would have inside information as to units becoming available and would pass that knowledge on to friends. If you were in the right place at the right time with money in your hand, in you went. There were dark jokes about dead bodies not yet cold before the next tenant was measuring her new casita for carpets.

Based on nothing, I decided that, after my lengthy wait on the list, my time surely was nigh. The area around the apartment that I had happily rented for six years on Calle Mesones had become increasingly noisy, and the rent was pinching my pocketbook. I was in search of a stopgap place to stay until the call came from La Quinta. At breakfast one Saturday morning in March, a chance remark from a friend led me immediately to Casa de los Soles, a small hotel/apartment complex ironically mere steps from La Quinta. I told Jorge, the middle-aged Mexican co-owner, along with his wife, Sandra, that I was on the waiting list at La Quinta and was looking for a temporary dwelling until my number came up and during the inevitable painting and furnishing phase of my new place. I spoke to Jorge only in Spanish, weak as it might have been, and I found him kind, friendly, and helpful. On a tour of the complex, we started by checking out some of the top-floor terraces, on one of which the freshly washed sheets and towels were drying on clotheslines in the abundant sun. I was smitten; this is something I really like. On another terrace, I was shown a little structure where a gardener made compost out of the fruit and vegetable waste of the tenants. *They had me at compost.*

Jorge then showed me a one-bedroom apartment on the second floor, and then, across the terrace, a three-bedroom, two-bath place with which I immediately fell madly in love. There was one problem, however: The larger place was already rented for the three winter months the following year, so I could not get into it until the next April, more than a year away. But, he asked me, would I consider renting the one-bedroom until the three-bedroom opened up, adding that if Quinta Loreto became available, of course all he would need would be a two-week notice for me to vacate whichever apartment I was in at that time.

Well yes, I would, gracias. Thus it was that when I left my apartment on Calle Mesones for the last time for my annual three months in Philadelphia—May, June, and July—I first took all of my belongings to Casa de los Soles, where they were put into its bodega until my return on August 1. On that date, my suitcases and boxes awaited me when I climbed the stairs to my new digs for the first of hundreds of times during the next eight months.

My apartment was small, there is no denying that, but it was cozy, had a full, attractive kitchen and plenty of storage space, and was very light and *muy tranquilo.* I adored the complex, its perfect location, and its charming owners and personnel. The reception area was staffed from 9 to 9 daily, with the door to the street locked up tight off-hours, accessible with the tenants' keys, of course, and a guard all night on Saturdays so that weekenders wouldn't bring any nonregistered guests in with them. I could count on the *chicos* at *recepción* for anything and everything: I could leave a book or a package for someone to pick up in my absence; they would accept deliveries for me and take them up to my apartment; they screened my visitors; they helped me with innumerable petty problems, usually of a technological nature; and included in my rent were a weekly cleaning and change of their bed linens and towels (it could have been twice a week, but I felt that was overkill), so that I didn't have to buy any. New garrafóns quickly replaced the old ones when they were empty—gratis.

The time in the small apartment went quickly and I was *muy contenta* there. When April 1st came around, all of my possessions were carried across the patio to my new home, the long-awaited three-bedroom apartment with no one above or below me. Meanwhile, there had been no email or call from Quinta Loreto telling me that my name had finally risen to the top of the list. After just one month in my new, much-larger place, I decided that Casa de los Soles would be my home for the foreseeable future, and I engaged the services of a fun interior-design couple, the Sublime Guys, to make the new apartment really mine. When I left again for my annual three-month Philly visit, their workers and Soles' employees flew into action, working side-by-side to completely repaint it, change all of the ceiling fixtures, make new thermal curtains for the windows and doors to the Juliet balconies off all three bedrooms, add area rugs, do some minor fixes here and there, and change out much of the art, turning my new quarters into a handsome, comfortable place I could happily call home.

It's easy to see why the place I live is called Casa de los Soles (House of the Suns).

I paid a visit to Georgina before I left town and told her to remove my name from the list, as I would not be coming to Quinta Loreto and was living around the corner instead. I have never regretted the decision that was actually made for me. I had wanted Quinta Loreto so much, but

I needed Casa de los Soles for my total peace of mind, comfort, happiness, and far less work and worry than I would have had if things had turned out another way.

Addendum: In late 2019, three and a half years after I first expressed interest, I received an email telling me that an apartment had opened up in Quinta Loreto and was I interested. I was not.

Getting My Space Heater to Work

It was the end of October and we were experiencing a really chilly spell. I needed to have the electric space heater that I had spied in the closet when I first saw the apartment the previous March. When I actually moved in in August, it was not there, as all of the heaters in all the apartments had been put away for the summer, I was told. I needed mine back, pronto. I made this request in the morning, and at dinnertime, one of the front-desk chicos came up to deliver it. I was thrilled! However, no instructions came with it in any language, either written or spoken, so later that evening, when the apartment was really starting to cool off, I sat down in front of the dials on the very-new-looking DeLonghi space heater, which reminded me of the radiators of my youth.

I figured out how to choose whether I wanted low, medium, or high heat, although I'd never seen a dial quite like that one, and I could choose #1 all the way up to #6 for the amount of heat, I guessed. Wasn't one of these dials redundant, offering the same thing, just in a different way? Then there was a dial with numbers on it. It being nighttime, and me being vision-challenged in the best of light, I assumed that the dial was to select the number of minutes I wanted heat. I turned the dial to 20. Then I put the plug into the socket, which I knew was working because the dials I had just set lit up red. I waited. No heat. I waited some more. No heat. I waited a full half hour and when there was still no heat,

I unplugged the machine, wrapped the cord around the holder for it, and put it near my door.

When I returned from yoga the next morning, I told Sandra, the co-owner of my complex, that my space heater didn't work and that I also needed a quilt (interestingly called an *edredón*—like eiderdown in English), as the blanket I had on my bed, while usually quite sufficient, was not up to the task in the extreme cold we were having. Sandra asked if I would like her to come right up and take a look at the space heater. I certainly would. So we wheeled the heater back into my bedroom and plugged it in. There we were, the two of us, squatting in front of the DeLonghi, squished into the narrow space between my bed and the wall, speaking in Spanish about how to make it give heat. I had to giggle a bit.

Sandra showed me that the dial with what I thought were minutes on it actually signified the 24 hours of the day. I went to get my magnifying glass to see that detail. Then she showed me that teensy, tiny pegs around the edge of the dial could be moved. Flat up and against the dial meant no heat; pulled away from the dial so that they were sticking out meant heat. Aha! Now I understood! Sandra pulled some of the pegs forward. No heat. Then I noticed a little arrow on the dial pointing to the number 10, and I said, *"La máchina no sabe que hora es. Pienso que es necesario para nosotros decir la máchina que hora es."* ("The machine does not know what time it is. I think that it is necessary for us to tell the machine what time it is.") I moved the dial so that the arrow faced 12, since it was high noon as we hunched down there. Then I pulled down many of the pegs after 12, going toward 13 (the heater uses a 24-hour system), and voilà—HEAT! I was so darned proud of myself to have figured this out once I had been given part of the necessary information on how to coax heat out of the DeLonghi.

Now all I need to do is to go buy a heavy-duty extension cord so that the heater will reach farther out into my living room/dining room/

kitchen area, as outlets are few and far between. And Sandra supplied me with the desired quilt, the same one that had been on the bed when I visited in March. I am now a warm and happy camper.

THE PRIVATIZATION OF TRASH COLLECTION IN SAN MIGUEL AND ITS FALLOUT

From the time I came to SMA in 2009, this is how trash was collected in El Centro, where I have always lived: A small truck (necessitated by the narrow 16th-century streets, which were never intended for 21st-century vehicles) would come around twice a week on a known schedule, preceded by a man jangling a triangle unbelievably loudly to signal the truck's approach. Doors all along the street were flung open, and housekeepers and homeowners rushed out with their trash bags, taking them to where the truck was parked for that particular block's pickup. The bags were tossed by the worker on the ground up to the other worker in the truck. Also high in the truck were enormous, heavy canvas bags into which recyclables were tossed by category by *"moscas"* ("flies"), men not on the city payroll but who provided a service by separating the items in the bags into glass, plastic, metal, paper and cardboard, and, finally, true trash. The moscas then sold the recycled goods to support their families, saving the city untold thousands of pesos a year in dumping fees.

This job was illegal, but no one ever intervened, which seems to be a pattern here. People generally do not interfere with another's efforts to make a living. I can think of the following examples: people getting onto buses and handing out free samples of peanuts, and a free bag to the bus driver for his indulgence, in the hope of selling a bag or two; people getting onto buses dressed as clowns and doing a short schtick with the aim of charming some riders into giving a tip; guitarists entertaining those on the bus for several blocks, looking for a few pesos in appreciation; or strolling musicians entering restaurants, offering to sing a song of the diners' choice for a fee.

Because the trucks were so small, they filled up quite rapidly and about once an hour they had to drive to the dump to unload what they had collected. It's a half hour each way from Centro to the dump, and while there, they had to wait in line with other small trucks to empty their load, thus there was a lot of downtime.

When I saw for myself and had confirmed that recyclables were indeed being separated from trash right on the truck, I started to collect them in separate bags in my apartment. When I had a full load, I gave the bag to the *conserje* (sort of translates to concierge, but without a similar meaning to English; a person doing the job of a combination of doorman, general maintenance worker, and helper with any task, also sometimes called a *mozo*) in my complex and he would then pass it on—already separated—to one of the moscas on the truck. I felt good knowing that my recyclables were actually being recycled and that I was assisting a man in supporting his family.

Fast-forward to late 2017: The city council of San Miguel decided, because of much-increased tourism and the resulting trash, to make a radical change in the way trash and recyclables are collected. The biggest change, and the one that informed all of the others, was that the city contracted with a private company to do the trash collection. Adorable mini trash compactors were purchased to replace the small open trucks of yore. As part of the compacting process, a clamshell closes down onto the many bags of unseparated trash, so that no men can be working up there. Poof—the moscas are out of a job and a living. Because of the compaction, the trucks need to go to the dump only about once in three to four hours, a great savings of time and gas. When the new trucks go to the dump and unload their cargo, a sea of people range over the mountains of debris and start separating out the recyclables and other things of value that might be resold.

Several other problems emerged with the new system: First, the private company did not hire all of the already-existing trash workers, so some men lost their jobs, although the ones who were hired got snappy blue and yellow uniforms. Next, the full fleet of trucks was not delivered on time and thus a smaller number of new trucks took on the nearly impossible task of picking up the trash from the same number of blocks as in the past. Also, the private company established new routes, with new pickup days and times, without communicating this to the homeowners. So, when no trash truck came at the usual time, trash bags were left outside of houses on sidewalks that were already laughably narrow, impeding walkers. Dogs sometimes got into these bags and left the block a mess. The headline in one issue of *Atención*, the local weekly newspaper, pleaded for patience with the trash situation, and the complaints did seem to die down, although I still see bags of trash on the sidewalk in various neighborhoods, something that had never been necessary before.

So how did this new system affect me? First, I was moving as these changes were taking place, although I still lived in Centro. When I went to my new place, I told Jorge that I was a fanatic about recycling and requested a number of small plastic trash cans in which to separate my cans, bottles, plastics, and paper suitable for recycling; they were cheerfully presented to me. I did this separating religiously for a number of months, but then became suspicious that all the items I had carefully separated were being dumped into one single bin, and it turned out I was correct. I spoke to Jorge about this and was told that they just didn't have room for separate containers for all manner of recyclables, and that now with the new system, there was no point to it, anyway. I was deeply distressed. Yes, I could continue to collect my recyclables and take a taxi out to the dump and give my bags directly to the former moscas, but I didn't quite see myself doing that for a variety of reasons.

Thus, I capitulated. I now throw everything into one trash can in my kitchen, and every time it is an item that I know could be recycled and bring income to a family, I cringe. One tiny saving grace is that a friend of mine, Jayne, does art projects with the kids in the campo who are dirt poor. I save things like wine corks ("We paint with them," says Jayne), toilet paper and paper towel tubes ("You wouldn't believe the adorable birds we make out of toilet paper tubes"), empty pill bottles to hold supplies of whatever, newspaper for papel-maché; you get the idea ("I'll take anything that can be used to make art").

I have found the most creative place to donate any clean plastic bags that I don't reuse at home: They go to a group that meets weekly at St. Paul's Episcopal Church that repurposes them into mattresses for kids in the campo who would otherwise sleep on the ground. Bags are twisted carefully into a tight ball (you need to be trained) and stuffed into heavy duck material—at about 1,000 plastic bags per mattress. (I do keep a few bags for garbage, which I stash in my freezer all week long because of my fear of ants or worse in the apartment; the housekeeper takes away the frozen garbage—to be added to the compost—on the day she cleans my apartment.)

I save any reusable takeout containers to give to Reyna, my former housekeeper, as she says her mother uses them to give leftovers to members of the large family who come for Sunday dinner. And the little plastic salad dressing containers with lids that come with the already-prepared salads I sometimes buy can go to my art-teacher friend to use as containers for paint for the kids to color those charming birds made out of toilet paper tubes.

So I've made my peace—more or less—with the disposition of the trash that I produce, but I always wish I could do more (and produce less).

BLOW UP JUDAS

This oddly named fiesta is an annual cathartic release for the Mexicans who have just come through a grueling *Semana Santa* (Holy Week). In the past, papel-mâché puppets of Judas were strung up and then blown up. In more recent times, the condemned are unpopular political figures. Today's pièce de résistance was The Donald. New this year on each figure are the names of the businesses that donated the doomed figures and to whom they are dedicated.

Here he is in all of his blond glory.
Underneath his name was a sign that said in Spanish, "But not the duck."

Even though there was a call not to sacrifice Donald Duck,
there he is on the right, in a cage, and he did get blown up. Not sure why.
Of course Donald Duck was never in a cage, but we won't quibble on details.

A witch was exploded, but her hat remained. Then a devil,
always a favorite to detonate, was destroyed.
Fittingly, the witch's hat, the devil's head, and Donald were all that were left.

After each subsequent figure was blown up, there were calls for The Donald to be next, but no, the people running this thing kept him for last to heighten the anticipation

With great glee, every eye and every camera, including mine of course,
was poised to capture this historic moment.

Donald was lowered for a few minutes so the debris in the street could be removed, and you should have heard the whistles and catcalls.

First he spun one way, with smoke pouring out, then the other.

There was a lengthy pause, then BOOM and he flew apart. There was nothing left but his blondness, and someone next to me said, "See, I knew there were no brains in there!"

All that remained of the Donald figure after it was exploded.

ONLY IN SAN MIGUEL

I've seen some interesting and/or funny T-shirts on Mexicans recently. I'm sure that in many cases they have no idea what the English words on the shirts say; they might have bought the garments from a pile of used clothing at *Tianguis* (the Tuesday Market) or a garage sale.

"Not now; I'm tanning!"

"I (heart) soccer moms"—this on a teenage boy.

"No, I won't fix your computer for you"—also on a teenage boy. Maybe he did know what it said.

"Is not my fart!"

I passed a Mexican woman wearing a T-shirt that said *"Trust Me, I'm Blonde."* And trust me, she wasn't.

Here's another T-shirt story: A large commercial bakery here (Wonder Bread-esque) is called Bimbo. All the bakery workers wear the shirts and they're even sold in stores. I always get a kick out of seeing a guy wearing a white shirt with bold red letters saying *"Bimbo."* Thank goodness they don't know what it means in English.

One day, I saw a workman with an orange safety vest and a yellow hard hat, obviously either going to work or returning home (at 1:30 on a Sunday afternoon, I have no idea which), and in addition to his work clothes, he was wearing a lavender Tinkerbell backpack with the words *"Follow the Pixie Dust."* I found this just hilarious, but I guess a backpack is a backpack when you need one.

With any home or community, there comes a time when its flaws can no
longer be ignored. In fact, this disillusion is part of growing up. ...Soon
enough, the vibrant colors of newness fade, and the complex realities
of the new home emerge alongside its original novelty and beauty.

"Home Is Where We Feel Connected" by Rev. Marisol Caballero,
from *Braver/Wiser,* Unitarian Universalist Association, 8/28/2019

CHAPTER 5

2018

WHATEVER IT IS I'M SEARCHING FOR, IT'S USUALLY HARD TO FIND

Yes, my love affair with San Miguel deepens with each passing year,
but I am no longer a starry-eyed newbie. Most of the things that
bother me are not huge problems by any means, just the cumulative
frustrations of a gringa who has not yet learned all she could about patience—I know for sure after 10 years that I was sent to Mexico to learn
patience—and these annoyances do, after all, make for good storytelling.
I must give up my desire to try to control situations that existed for years
before I appeared on the scene, and I need to let long-accepted ways of
doing things in this culture—not my comfort level nor my ideas of how
things could be improved—guide my actions and reactions.

Time of course does not stand still in SMA—that's impossible
anywhere, really—but with its colonial architecture, cobblestone streets,
and nostalgic fiestas and tourism marketing reminding one that SMA
is the birthplace of the movement for independence from the Spanish
conquerors, I occasionally believed that in some strange way nothing
would ever change in this magical city. But things always have changed

and they always will, and the transformations won't all be for the better and won't please everyone. I loved SMA so much just the way I discovered it that I selfishly wanted it all to remain the same.

Finding an Old Friend at His New Location

In the spring, I was working with my book designer, Margot, at her SMA apartment for a couple of weeks before she returned to Canada. At one of our weekly appointments, she let me know that a photo she wanted to use in the book was not in the proper format. That night, I emailed Gerardo, the owner of ArtPrint, the company I've been using for my photographic needs, to ask him to fix the photo I would be sending to him. I was going to give him a week to respond and do the work, knowing that he had just moved the location of his business, a pretty big deal for an operation like his.

Because Margot's place is very close to ArtPrint's new venue, after my next meeting with her, I went looking for it. Once I walked up and down both sides of several blocks of Calzada de la Aurora, noting that the numbers made absolutely no sense, odds and evens on both sides, and not in any particular order that I could discern, I started asking people. I told them that it was a photography studio, that it was called ArtPrint, and that it was #12. Nobody had a clue, and some sent me off on a couple of wild-goose chases.

I went into the unmarked office between #11 and #13, thinking maybe it was #12, and a worker there had no idea at what address she was working. Then I started in again on the side with San Sebastian Bakery (a landmark Margot surmised was near to where she thought #12 should be). When I saw a man who runs an art gallery taking boxes out to a delivery person, I asked him, and he knew! ArtPrint is in the former Hansen's restaurant location, with which I am familiar!

So I went in, found Gerardo, and congratulated him on the move, and he told me they hadn't had phone or Internet service since then. He said he goes out several times a day to an Internet cafe and downloads all of his emails, then comes back to the office and reads them. He found the one from me and he said he'd have it out to us by that night. I wasn't convinced, but at least it's now on his radar.

Gerardo told me he had not yet received permission to put up a sign. The sign has to be approved because it's a historic area. He told me what he had gone through with the phone and Internet companies to try to establish service and with the government office that approves signs. It turned down his first sign, so then he took photos of his neighbors' signs to show that his was very similar. That office will be working only Monday and Tuesday next week as it's Semana Santa, so who knows when he will be able to put up his sign. There is a small #12 on a set-back wall on his building, but if he'd had an ArtPrint sign up, I would have found him right away, in spite of the fact that #12 is not in any order along that block.

Then I told him about the errors on Google when Margot and I looked him up to get his new address. (It truncated the name of his street, and his hours are listed as "Closing hours, 9:00 a.m.-5 p.m.") Of course he can't fix them as he has no Internet. He said that there would be a big ad in *Atención* next week stating the new locale and that there was a sign on the door at the old location. I told him that in subsequent ads, he should state that it's in the old Hansen's restaurant spot, because a lot of gringos know that location.

LAUNDRY WOES

Boy, do I have laundry stories to tell! Until fairly recently, I always had the luxury of at least a washer (and sometimes even a dryer) in whatever apartment I was renting at the time. But in my new abode, where there is neither, I have had to figure out how to get my dirty clothes clean. There are no self-serve laundromats in SMA that I know of; they all have attendants who do your laundry for you at an incredibly low price, which of course includes water, detergent, electricity for the washing machine, gas for the dryer, folding, and salaries for the attendants. I don't know how they do it.

When I first moved to my new neighborhood last April, I found a really nice laundry. It was on Calzada de la Luz and the attendant's name was Luz de Maria, which I found amusing. She was a sweetheart until … I took in two bags of laundry, one whites, one colors, and asked her NOT to wash them together. But she did, probably to save on water and/ or soap, electricity, and space in the washer and dryer. When I got them back, two of my favorite white blouses were gray, as was my underwear. I was so angry, I couldn't speak. Soon afterward, that laundry closed and Luz was out of a job. But I had learned a valuable lesson: Never take colors and whites to a lavandería at the same time. What I do is take a bag of one color, and when I pick it up, I leave a bag of the other color.

So I tried another laundry that is on a route I take almost daily. When I went to pick up my first finished load, my ticket was in a bag with someone else's laundry, which caused me to panic, as someone might, in turn, have my laundry. Some hapless person might have picked it up, never even looking to see if it was theirs. Then the quite-aged attendant brought me several other loads to look at. Nope. Finally, she invited me into the laundry itself and asked me to look at the piles of finished, bagged laundry and try to find mine. I did, but that was the end of my association with that laundry facility.

After some asking around about locations and reputations of laundries, I finally found a good, dependable one with which I was very comfortable. It was ideal because it was on the way to and from my yoga classes when they were on Calle Organos, but soon thereafter the location of my yoga classes changed. What I've come to think of as "my" laundry is not so far from my apartment, but it now means a special trip just to take and pick up my clothes.

One Saturday, I saw that the lavandería almost directly across the street from the Hotel Posada Aldea, to which my yoga classes have moved and where my UU congregation meets, was open on Sundays. I thought: *This is the answer! I can take or pick up my laundry on any of four days a week. It's right on my route.* So, Sunday, I took in a load and the attendant said something to me that I totally didn't understand. I asked her to repeat what she said; I still didn't get it. What could she possibly be telling me that I couldn't understand? She then pointed to a sign on the wall that said in Spanish, "Esteemed Clients — For hygiene reasons we are no longer washing underwear." Since everything in my load except for a couple of towels was underwear, I just stood there with my mouth hanging open. How do they have any customers at all? What are you supposed to do with your underwear, take it to a separate laundry? I then had to drag my dirty laundry to church, and then schlep it back home, which made it impossible for me to buy the fruits and veggies I was going to stock up with on my return trip since I couldn't carry both them and my laundry bag.

When I took that same load of laundry to my tried-and-true lavandería near where I used to take yoga, right near the dropoff/pickup counter was a hanger with about a dozen single socks clipped to it. These were socks that didn't go home with their owners for one reason or another. Since I had a missing sock, I looked through the collection, but, alas, it was not there. I thought it was clever, though—and kind—of the attendants to hang up the strays in the hopes that their owners would claim them. Since then, I have bought small mesh bags into which I put all of my soiled socks and secure the openings, and in that way, none of my socks will end up on the hanger or be lost forever, but will be returned to me intact and in pairs.

Another day, I went to retrieve my clean laundry from that same place, and after I presented my ticket, the attendant looked high and low for my plastic bag. I told her it was all dark colors to save her time looking at everything. You wouldn't believe what she had to do. The lavandería is a very long, narrow space, and above the two washers and two dryers and on a part of the opposite wall are shelves on which to put the bags of clean laundry. On the floor across from the machines sit the bags of dirty laundry, awaiting their turn, leaving maybe two feet of space for the attendants to walk back and forth. This woman had to open up and get onto a stepstool to climb on top of one of the washers to look through the stacks of bags for mine. She did this at least three times. Mine was definitely not there. My heart was sinking, as my load had contained a quite-new, pretty-expensive bathrobe that I had bought on vacation in Canada last fall.

When the attendant said that she was going to go upstairs, I figured it was to look at whatever bags were stored up there. A minute later, she came back down with her cellphone and called the teenager who had received my dirty laundry the previous day. She is acquainted with me and immediately told the older woman where my clean laundry was. It was upstairs with the blankets, whatever the heck that means, and why mine was there, I will never know. There were no blankets in my load. When the older woman came back down carrying my bag, she had a big grin on her face and I relaxed. Just another laundry day in Mexico....

I wrote the poem that follows during COVID, two years after the rest of these laundry stories. But since it was relevant to the topic, I thought I'd add it here. I believe it is self-explanatory.

A Singular Heroine

In the hierarchy of boring, unpleasant jobs,
    working in a laundry has to be near the top of the list.
Clothes in all stages of filth are brought in
    to be handled by women with few other options.
It's essential work, but soul-sucking and repetitive,
    and yet, at my lavandería in San Miguel, it is done well.
I am met with a smile and a greeting.
I am thanked when I produce exact change.
I am wished a *buen día* when I leave.
And the clothes are beautifully folded,
    all the panties with the other panties,
        the socks with the socks—all part of the job.
But, the laundry chica, far down on the pecking order,
    proved herself a tower of a person
    when, in these treacherous times,
She tucked the 200-peso note I inadvertently left in a pants pocket
    into my bag of clean laundry.
I never would have known.
She didn't say a word,
    probably had forgotten about it by the time I picked up my clothes.
But I will never forget it.

The next time that I went to the laundry, I handed the same attendant an envelope in which were the 200 pesos ($10 USD) and a short
note in Spanish thanking her for her character and honesty in returning the money to me. Several months later, when I was again picking
up my clean clothes, I saw some papers on top of one of the washers
that looked like those that would be used to teach first-graders how to

form the letters of the alphabet, so I asked the now familiar attendant if she was a *maestra* (teacher). She said that she was, but that because of COVID there was no in-person school, and so she was working at the family business—the lavandería—instead of hiring a chica. So much for my elitist assumption that the pleasant woman who washes my clothes and returned my money had no other options and was at the bottom of the work totem pole for women. I have since seen other members of her family working there: her husband and two teenage children, one a boy. I now know that this is probably an enlightened, well-educated family, as even the male members were working at the lavandería.

I Am (Unwitting) Entertainment for My Neighbors

One October day, I provided entertainment for a group of people shopping at the Artisans' Market, which is very close to my apartment at Casa de los Soles. A friend who lives at La Quinta Loreto, which is right around the corner from my place, and I took a cab home from a fantastic lecture about cancer vaccines that the visiting scientist was working on and which she thought would be standard procedure in about 15 years, so that the following generations will not have to battle cancer. Since there was no bus after quite a lot of waiting, we hopped into a cab. We got out somewhere between Soles and the driveway up to La Quinta and were standing there talking for a long time, she facing Soles and I facing away.

There is an *Elote* (corn on the cob) Man with a cart who boils corn and walks the streets hawking it around dinnertime. He has a most unusual and incredibly loud bellow. It took me months before I figured out that he was saying "elote" in seemingly about 10 syllables, elongating the final one to incredible lengths. Several more months went by until I was able to isolate the words for his other products, "*esquites*" (corn cut off the cob), "*cacahuates*" (peanuts), and "garbanzos" (chickpeas). That evening, he let out one of those signature booming cries, and since I wasn't facing him, it came as a complete surprise. I have a hearing condition where, even though I am going deaf (slowly, but surely), loud sounds seem even louder to me than they actually are. That shout caused me to jump so much that everyone around was laughing. One of the chicos working at reception at Soles was hanging out at the doorway, and several other Mexicans who were around really cracked up. Glad I could be the source of such merriment!

My jumpiness isn't the only way I've made people laugh here. I have been looking for tiny stick-on bows for the little plastic zip-top bags in which I have placed the Mujeres en Cambio logo earrings that I sell for that scholarship organization. The place from which I bought them for years doesn't seem to have them anymore, and even though the owner says she's ordering them ("mañana"), they are never in, so yesterday, I tried another *papelería* (stationery store, broadly interpreted). I entered and asked for *monos chiquititos* (what I thought I was saying was "tiny little bows"). The clerk, a woman about my age, gave me a peculiar look and asked me what I wanted to do with the monos chiquititos, and I described them as having tape on the bottom so that one can stick them on a miniature gift. Oh, she says, *moños* (the correct word for bows). I had asked for little, tiny monkeys! I well know the word for monkeys in Spanish, but somehow forgot to add the tilde (accent mark over the "n" to change it to an "ñ") in my pronunciation to make the word "bows." We both dissolved into laughter. It was a very sweet moment, and no, she didn't have them.

As I left her store, she was still doubled over the counter, holding her stomach and laughing. I am sure she and her family had another good chuckle that night at the dinner table when she relayed her encounter with me. I find that these types of interchanges are the most endearing, when I, in my earnest attempt to speak Spanish, am the source of a shared pleasurable experience—laughter, when I truly know that the Mexicans are not laughing at me but with me.

Another incident like this took place when I was out to lunch with dear friends, Eduardo and Alejandra. We were talking about exercising, and I showed them my new Fit-Bit, announcing in Spanish that it measured my *pasas* (raisins). Again there was a stunned look until they figured out that what I had meant to say was *pasos* (steps).

And, I'm happy to say, this occasionally goes both ways. At a hairdresser's appointment one day, Miguelina asked me if I wanted her to use the "eraser" on my hair. Now it was my turn to look puzzled. When I put my glasses on to see what she might be holding to use on my head, I saw that it was a razor, and I quickly understood how those two similar-sounding words could have confused her.

FUNERAL

The other day I experienced a heartbreaking funeral procession. The mourners were walking slowly and silently without any musical accompaniment, which was unusual. They were on Ancha de San Antonio (*ancha* means wide, and this is one of the very few four-lane streets in San Miguel, two of which are given over to precious parking) as it leads to the cemetery that I visit on Day of the Dead.

The first thing I noticed when I saw the group of about 25 people was that they all carried white balloons, something I'd not seen before. Then I was startled and saddened to see—at the front of the line—presumably the father, carrying on his shoulder a not even 24-inch-long coffin covered in white satin, held in place by his upraised hand.

I have seen these diminutive caskets in the window of the coffin store next door to the Bonanza market along with adult-sized ones in different polished woods, and they always cause me to reflect on the need for a family to have to buy one of those. Mexicans do not shrink from death. They have their Day of the Dead fiestas each year, and a store is selling coffins on a main street next to a mini-supermarket. I like their relationship to death.

Since by law in Mexico all deceased persons must be cremated or buried within 24 hours, I knew that the procession of mourners must have been in the very early stages of grief at the death of a baby, and I watched as they walked slowly and sorrowfully out of my sight to bury their beloved tiny one. I wondered when the balloons would be released to the sky—as the coffin was lowered into the minuscule grave or when the last shovelful of earth was placed on top of it, and then the grieving parents and other relatives would mournfully retrace their footsteps home.

ANOTHER TYPE OF PROCESSION

One Saturday afternoon late, I saw the strangest sight. It was a large group of exquisitely dressed wedding guests parading down the Ancha presumably from the just-concluded wedding ceremony in the parroquia to the reception many blocks away at the Instituto Allende. The women were all wearing flip-flops (certainly not the most practical footwear for San Miguel's cobbled streets) and carrying their sky-high heels (an even worse choice!) in see-through plastic bags.

CHANGES, CHANGES, AND MORE CHANGES

In the nine years that I have been visiting and then living in San Miguel, I have seen monumental alterations, transformations, mutations, call them what you will; in my opinion, they are not all for the better. After the city received UNESCO's World Heritage Site designation in 2009, readers' surveys in glossy travel magazines—one by one—began to name it the most beautiful city in the world (had none of them visited Paris?), the best small city in the world, and the friendliest city in the world. Mexico's traditional cuisine was included in UNESCO's Intangible Cultural Heritage of Humanity, and this year, the International Bureau of Cultural Capitals named San Miguel the Cultural Capital of the Americas for 2019. The city tourist board pulled its international advertising pesos back in-country and Mexican tourists began to come in droves.

The infrastructure of the town cannot support this influx of cars, many of them huge, nor the hordes of people who arrive in them. On weekends and holidays in particular, there is an almost-constant state of gridlock on the mostly narrow, one-way, cobbled 16th-century streets. The cramped sidewalks are often impassable with the addition of tourists' baby strollers. It's very difficult to get a taxi or a restaurant reservation on the weekends. I have a new modus operandi since this multitude descended. If I can't walk to an event on the weekend, I will not attend it, as snagging a cab is nearly impossible, and if it's raining, all hope is lost. I always have the expectation that it will be a performance that will be repeated during the less-crowded weekdays, and if not, so be it.

The taxi drivers hate the crowds. They can't make any money as they sit in long lines of traffic, burning gas, when ordinarily they could transport several fares in the same time period. I have frequently exited a taxi far from my destination, choosing to walk the rest of the way rather than sitting in a traffic jam showing no signs of moving.

Luxury hotels and high-end restaurants with valet parking are popping up all over. A sizable number of venerable restaurants have sold their valuable properties or lost their leases, closed altogether, or moved out of town. It is so distressing to witness this domino fall of beloved tiendas and restaurantes, to be supplanted by hip, in some cases vulgar, new establishments catering to a far different clientele from that of the past.

Expensive boutiques now dazzle in places where there was formerly a huge, beloved hardware store, and other tiendas catering to the locals are being edged out in favor of these fashionable establishments. Rules have been put in place about where the Indigenous selling their crafts on the street should limit themselves. And there is unchecked construction that has left some hideous and poorly constructed apartment buildings as eyesores in the hills surrounding the city.

Many plans have been floated to alleviate the pollution, the lack of mobility on streets and sidewalks, the exponentially larger amount of trash generated, an increase in petty crime, and all the other problems that surface when too many people are in a space unprepared to deal with them. The idea of virtual parking meters in El Centro, along with the elimination of parking spaces in front of homes where the owners have always been allowed to park, was suggested, and a demonstration against it quickly quashed that idea. Another suggestion was a series of parking lots at all entrances to the city, with free or very low-cost electric buses taking tourists into El Centro, creating a walking-only environment there.

While this sounds promising, there are potential problems with the elderly and handicapped, those who will have a great deal of luggage, and those who insist on parking very close to their hotel or restaurant. Nothing has happened that I'm aware of to move this potentially workable plan forward to completion, except that some spiffy nonelectric buses run into and out of Centro almost totally empty on a regular basis. The city is frequently just plain overwhelmed. I have read articles that say that these types of problems are a common occurrence with places that have garnered the World Heritage Site designation.

And then there is the water crisis. The Independence Aquifer runs under most of the state of Guanajuato, where San Miguel is located. For about a decade, scientists and water engineers have been warning that the amount of rain we've been getting has not been sufficient to refill the aquifer because of the enormous quantity of water that is being taken out annually by agribusiness, whose crops are mostly for export (I have heard that 85 percent of the water used is for this endeavor); that the aquifer is alarmingly low; and that the remaining water is fossil groundwater containing dangerously high levels of arsenic and fluoride. Communities in the campo who have no access to any other water are paying a high price, as their children's bodies absorb these chemicals at a higher rate than adults', resulting in physical and mental abnormalities, permanently brown teeth, reduced cognitive abilities, and other horrors. And yet, given this scenario, new developments of hundreds of houses at a time are sprouting up like mushrooms with no end in sight.

Located as SMA is in the *bajio* (heartland) of Mexico, we sometimes see on our streets filthy, starving travelers who have taken a break from riding atop "*la bestia*" ("the beast," the freight train) on their way from their desperate, dangerous, insecure lives, in Central America mostly, to the U.S. And coming from the other direction are Mexican nationals who have been deported from the States. Frequently these newcomers to our town are accompanied by their families, which often include babies and small children. My UU congregation reacted to the deportees by establishing Caminamos Juntos (We Walk Together), a nonprofit to aid the returnees in whatever they need: housing, jobs, schooling for the children, Spanish lessons (yes, many who have lived their whole lives in the U.S. know little or no Spanish), acculturation, and the list goes on. It is funded by the congregation, individual donations, fundraisers, and a large grant from the Southern Region of the Unitarian Universalist Association.

Friends of mine established another nonprofit, the Latin American

Relief Fund (LARF), in support of Alberque ABBA House, a temporary place of respite in the nearby town of Celaya for migrants where they can stay and rest for three days and nights, take showers, get new clothes and shoes, eat three healthy meals a day, learn about their legal rights, get medical care and psychological counseling, and obtain a raft of other services. Because of the many who have become amputees, losing a leg or arm after a fall or a push from the train, ABBA House now has a specialized facility for these folks. It is the only such facility in the country. LARF is funded by individual donations, fundraisers, and grants.

On a more personal level, many friends—for a variety of reasons, including the aforementioned changes to San Miguel, increasing age, health issues, and wanting to be with grandchildren—are selling their homes and belongings and leaving SMA altogether, or moving out to the countryside where life is calmer. Simply stated, things are not what they were when I arrived in 2009. On the plus side...well, the hospitality industry is thriving, more jobs have been created, and vendors do sell more goods to the thousands of tourists than they did to the smaller crowds, but at what price? While I watch all of these changes and adapt my life in some ways to accommodate them, I wonder where they will end, and where I will be in the future. Honestly, I can think of no other place in the world with the unique makeup of San Miguel with its stunning weather, preserved colonial architecture, and fascinating history as the cradle of Mexican independence.

THEN ALONG CAME PING

I mentioned earlier that I would be living for about nine months in a tiny though totally sufficient-for-me one-bedroom apartment in Casa de los Soles, a small hotel/apartment complex on Calle Loreto, as I await the vacancy of the three-bedroom, two-bath apartment I have my eye on there. During the nine months of the year that aren't the "high season" here, most of the guests are Mexican weekenders. Some of them have wound up in the apartment above mine, and that hasn't always been so good for me. First there was the man who snored so loudly that he woke me from a deep sleep in the middle of the night—and I was wearing ear plugs. He also made disgusting throat and nose noises in his bathroom in the mornings upon awakening, which, since the weather was warm when he was renting, I could hear clearly through the jalousie window in my bathroom (which opens onto an air duct into which his window undoubtedly also opens). But then, after the weekend, he left. He returned several times, but he always left in a couple of days.

Then there was the man (I don't know if it was a man, but I am imagining that it was) who smoked pot in his room atop mine day and night, and those same open jalousie windows on both the third and second floors allowed that acrid odor to permeate my apartment. I was in a moral dilemma as to how to handle it—talk to him, complain to the owners, suck it up—when he left.

And a woman in high heels moved in one weekend and proceeded to click her way back and forth across the ceramic tile floors for hours until she left to go out. She also vacated on Sunday.

As high season—January, February, and March—neared, I became very worried that one of these types or another equally disturbing one would move in for the entire season, as many of the guests do at my complex during those months. Then along came Ping.

One day as I was going out my door, a woman came down from the third-floor apartment, and after introducing herself as Ping, asked if she were making too much noise. I thought I had died and gone to heaven. I responded, "Not yet." Ping is a tiny Canadian woman and makes absolutely no noise of any kind. Occasionally I could hear a bit of the sound of her TV, but only in the bedroom, and it didn't interfere with my getting to sleep. Once, she brought me a container of delicious vegetarian stew that she made "too much of" and needed to share. This was Ping's 16th winter in this complex. When she first started coming, the owners' son was in kindergarten; he is now in university. Every time I told someone where I lived, they would say, "Oh, you must know Ping!"

I was so lucky to have someone like Ping directly above me, especially now that I know what it might have been like under other circumstances. I might have had to move, depending on what was going on daily and nightly above me. Each day, I gave thanks for the presence of Ping in the upstairs apartment. When winter was over and Ping ended her stay at Casa de los Soles, I moved across the patio to the larger apartment I'd been waiting for, with no one living on top of nor below me.

SHOPPING, MEXICAN-STYLE

In April 2018, I moved into my long-awaited three-bedroom, two-bath apartment in Centro, and while I was out of the country for three months that summer, I had it considerably altered. I returned to it on August 1 but didn't have my first houseful of guests until mid-October, making me realize that I needed luggage stands on which to place suitcases rather than on the beds, and also freestanding towel racks, as there was not sufficient room to hang the wet towels of guests in the bathrooms. Thus, I began a search for these two items, never dreaming it would become a quest.

I started locally with La Comer and Bodega Aurrera (Walmart, I'm embarrassed to say). I hopefully attended garage and estate sales, all to no avail, then I thought of going to Costco in Celaya, about an hour away. I needed to go with someone who had both a car and a Costco card, as I have neither. My friend Ellen had both and invited me to join her on a trip to Costco one Sunday. We got an early start, before 10 a.m., and had high hopes of reaching Celaya before the usual weekend crowds at Costco materialized. Alas, at about five miles away from Celaya, we ran into a pilgrimage for San Judas de Tadeo.

The veneration of Judas Thaddaeus in Mexico has taken on importance since the mid-20th century. Judas Thaddaeus (or San Judas Tadeo in Spanish) was one of the Twelve Apostles. A relative of Jesus', he was one of his first followers and after Jesus' death became an evangelizer. He was martyred by decapitation with a hatchet. He is considered to be a direct intercessor to Jesus as a saint to appeal to in tough and desperate circumstances and is credited with many miracles. Petitions often include help with personal situations, legal problems, work issues, and family. Sometimes the petition might simply be that the state of affairs does not get any worse. Veneration of San Judas receives support from the Catholic Church as a manifestation of folk religion in Latin America.

On the 28th of each month, masses are held in honor of this saint, and some will walk the entire way from their homes to the church, starting the night before. Most attendees have images of the saint with them from their homes, which can be anywhere from eight inches to over six feet in height, made of various materials. Those with small children sometimes dress them as the saint. For this monthly event, police are assigned to the area around the church, mostly to direct traffic.

While this saint is venerated every single month, we hit the jackpot on October 28, the saint's feast day. Thousands upon thousands of people were walking along the shoulders of both sides of the four-lane highway to reach a central meeting place where the adoration took place. Many carried small children and statues of various sizes of the saint, and some of the children and an occasional adult were dressed like San Judas. There were vendors galore, selling food and beverages, candles, rosaries, T-shirts, and, of course, religious objects, including statues of the saint, some of which we saw still in their original plastic wrappers in the arms of their buyers. Things were pretty chaotic, as an ambulance and various police cars pulled up on the shoulder, and pedestrians were constantly crossing the road for reasons we didn't understand, weaving in and out of the nearly motionless traffic. Ellen's car began to overheat and I had nightmare visions of it stalling on this highway that had become a parking lot. But I was actually pleased that we had something interesting to gawk at as we sat and fumed.

We reached Costco almost two and a half hours after we left SMA. By then, of course, the shoppers were there in force. Our first order of business was to replace Ellen's stolen Costco card, the process for which went quickly. Although we were very hungry, the new card was needed to buy food at the huge, efficient eating area outside. We each had one of the fabulously delicious all-beef, foot-long (I kid you not) hot dogs with a variety of self-serve condiments that I had been hearing about from regular Costco shoppers for years. For 30 pesos (about $1.50 USD), you got a hot dog and a soda with unlimited refills.

After eating, we started walking around the cavernous store pushing enormous grocery carts. Ellen bought quite a bit of food, and I looked searchingly for luggage and towel racks. I was ultimately disappointed; there were none to be found.

Since I had a birthday party to attend starting at 4 p.m., we did not have time to go to Ellen's other desired destination, Home Depot. We debated returning the way we had come, but since at that point it was only 3 p.m., we decided that it would be the same stop-and-go traffic going back, so we took an alternate return route with which Ellen was familiar. That turned out to be extremely scenic and without any traffic at all, but very long, and we arrived in SMA around 4:45.

That night, when I returned from the party, I decided to try to order the items from amazon.com.mx. It had the things I wanted, although one would have to be shipped from the U.S., but at that point,

I was willing to pay the shipping costs and the duty. The items went into my cart, but the site would not accept the credit card that I had on file with amazon.com. I thought maybe it was because I never use my credit card in Mexico and thus didn't let VISA know that I was in Mexico. I needed to do that, and I did. Still, my credit card was rejected. Someone later told me that it probably wanted a Mexican credit card, which I don't have.

Then I tried the U.S. version, amazon.com. It also had the needed items but wouldn't ship one of them to Mexico. So on Tuesday, I made a trip to La Luciernaga (which strangely enough means "glow worm" in Spanish), a shopping mall on the outskirts of SMA, and went directly to the Liverpool department store. I took printouts from my laptop of both a luggage stand and a towel rack, because even though I had looked up the names of these items online in Spanish, I thought it best to have a pictorial representation. Indeed, in the towel department, a pleasant young man, although not the sharpest knife in the drawer, went online and showed me all of the racks of both kinds that Liverpool carried. I didn't like any of the ones for towels, but being desperate at this point with my entire family coming for Christmas in less than two months, I chose one, and the clerk determined that two were indeed available in stock. I paid for them, getting a 20 percent discount as it was the store's anniversary month, and he went to fetch them from inventory.

As I was waiting, up high and to my left I saw a display with a beautiful wooden towel rack, draped with very attractive towels, and I was immediately smitten with it—it was exactly what I wanted! When Alejandro (we were on a first-name basis by this point) returned with two boxes, I asked him, in Spanish, of course, as the entire conversation so far had been, if the rack in the towel display was for sale. He assured me that it was. But, I said, I did not see that towel rack on the store's website that you showed me. You are right, señora, he said. I did not pursue that line of questioning. I told Alejandro that I wanted the towel rack that was on display and to put the money I had paid for the ones I didn't like toward the one I loved. Alejandro brought down the already-assembled one that had been on display and then left again to find another one in inventory. He returned with one in a box and we went through the transaction.

I had liked one of the luggage stands online, but they were not in stock, so I had to order them, and they could be delivered directly to my *habitación* gratis, so I then paid for them, and he called for a porter to help me get the towel racks out to a taxi.

When I got the items home, I asked the chico on duty at recepción, Paco, if he would put the boxed towel rack together for me, and I showed him the already-assembled one to use as a guide. Success! I swooned with happiness and awaited breathlessly the arrival in 10 days to two weeks of my two luggage racks, which appeared right on schedule.

THE LAST LEAVING

As 2018 crept toward its end, my whole visiting family piled one day into a BajioGO van to ride from San Miguel de Allende to the Querétaro airport for a flight to the beach resort Puerto Escondido. On our way up the Libramiento, we passed the outsized waterfowl—duck? goose? swan?—on top of a house below, and a lively discussion broke out over its raison d'être in a colonial Mexican city that holds the distinction of being a UNESCO World Heritage Site. But while voices and opinions swirled around me, I was struck with a thought: What if this were my last trip to the Querétaro airport? What if I were leaving San Miguel, not for a week at the beach, not for my customary three months in the States, but for the last time? Tears filled my eyes, and the road swam before me. I had to consider the possibility, nay the probability, that one day frailness or ill health would no longer permit me to walk San Miguel's challenging streets and would force me to take this ride for the final time. Would I by then use a walker or be pushed in a wheelchair? At the airport, would I be delivered to the front of every line? Would someone other than I hand my passport and boarding pass to the agent? Would I be among the first to board the plane? Would someone stow my carry-on and make sure I was settled in my seat with seatbelt tightly fastened?

Would I cry copious tears and would people stare at me? Surely some might guess why I was leaving, but could anyone know what and whom I was leaving? My perfect apartment on Calle Loreto, practically next door to the Artisans' Market with its hand-embroidered blouses and tailored shirts that made any man look dashing; highly polished necklaces, bracelets, and earrings—*Es plata, señora* (It's silver, señora)— carefully and lovingly placed just so each day in hopes of appreciative customers; its decorated mirrors, catrina T-shirts, ceramic bowls, little beaded purses, and a thousand other treasures waiting to be discovered; and farther up a long flight of stairs, tantalizing piles of peppers, mangoes, apples, tomatoes, and other fruits and vegetables I have never tasted and know not their names, next to brilliant bouquets of wild, extravagant flowers that beguile the eyes.

Would they know I was taking my ultimate leave from daunting cobblestones that had been trod by sandals and boots for half a millennium; not-very-melodic church bells that had awakened families for eons; noisy, smelly buses with teenage drivers on cellphones and the Virgen de Guadalupe for protection; taxis that always stopped to let a pedestrian cross; bride and groom mojiganga puppets striding down the street to an event; children selling *chicles*; Indigenous vendors peddling their charming crafts; beggars rasping *"Por el amor de Díos"* over outstretched palms?

Had they sipped a ginger margarita or savored an order of enchiladas verdes con pollo, talked with a friend over a glass of freshly squeezed limonada or tasted a slice of cool tres leches cake?

Did they know the joy of being welcomed and accepted in a foreign land, the warmth of many smiles, so many *abrazos* (hugs) and *besos* (kisses), shy glances from curious toddlers?

And the music, had they heard the music—from the mariachis to the opera singers, from the guitarist on the bus strumming and singing for a few pesos to the tuxedoed countertenor on the stage in the auditorium singing "Ave Maria" from deep within his soul, the jazz, the blues, the Cuban rhythms, drums, trumpets, brilliant solos played by international favorites on a world-class piano, the one-legged woman sitting on a stool on the street playing a battered one-stringed guitar?

Had they smelled the exhaust from too many gridlocked cars dropping off too many tourists; had they seen the past nibbled away bit by bit by bit as swank replaced history and glitz overcame adobe?

Did they see the abundant flowers—cascading bougainvillea in many hues, *nochebuena* (poinsettia) plants for Christmas, tons and tons of marigolds for decorating altars and graves for Day of the Dead?

I did all of those things and had those experiences. I shivered and I sweated, laughed and cried. I bought and I donated. I worked and played, wrote and read. And I walked and walked and walked. And I learned, endlessly. I, a gringa in perilous times, was privileged to live in San Miguel de Allende, in the bajio of Mexico, and I loved it. And I believe—no, I know—that it loved me back.

Only in SMA

On the seven-minute walk to my thrice-weekly yoga classes at their former location, I saw the same man every time on Calzada de la Luz, a road along an *arroyo* (a steep-sided gully cut by running water), walking multiple dogs on leashes. I watched him responsibly pick up the dogs' poop in plastic bags, and I felt so good until I then—with horror—saw him throw those same plastic bags through an opening in the concrete barrier into the arroyo. I still wonder if he thought he was doing the right thing.

"Tell me, what is it you plan to do with *your* one wild and precious life?"

Mary Oliver

CHAPTER 6

2019

WHEN SADNESS OVERTAKES ME, JOY OR SURPRISE REDEEMS ME

The beginning of this year marks the start of my 11th year in Mexico. My skin shows the effects of living for this length of time in the high desert. I continue to make adjustments for my age. San Miguel no longer feels like a foreign country; it's just where I live. Yet now and then, surprising, sometimes distressing, often heartwarming things happen, and I feel compelled to record them. The stories in this chapter fall into each of these categories.

JANUARY

DOWNED CABLES

One day as I was nearing my apartment at Casa de los Soles on Calle Loreto, I noticed the trash truck coming for its thrice-weekly pickup. This was one of the new trash trucks that a private waste collection company had been using since it was hired to take over trash collection in the city. These trucks have a clamshell design so the top can open to accept bags of trash and then close to compact it. The truck I saw was coming down the street with the clamshell open, and I was shocked to see it pull down many thick cables from overhead. Once they saw what was happening, the trash workers removed the cables manually from the truck's top and let them fall to the sidewalk. All the witnesses to this just stood in place gaping at the destruction.

Later in the afternoon, two men with ladders picked up the fallen cables and draped them over the balconies of the houses lining the street in that spot. I didn't know if the men were from the cable company or were just good neighbors helping out.

That night, we didn't have any Internet, which is unusual where I live. The outage continued into the next morning. I was sure it was because of the downed cables from the day before. I went to reception in my apartment complex to inquire what was being done and was told that Internet service would be restored in about a half hour, and indeed it was. I returned to reception to thank them for getting service restored so promptly and told of my hypothesis that the interruption in service was caused by the trash truck pulling down all the cables in that small area. I turned and pointed to where the cables had been dislodged and was dumbfounded to see that they were completely gone. There were no more cables of any kind on that side of the street. Incredulous, I asked the chico on duty what had happened to the cables and was told that when the company came out to investigate, it found that those were old cables that no longer functioned. They were taken down and hauled away. I can't tell you how different and much better it looked with those ugly, very thick cables removed. So, actually, the trash truck did the neighborhood a huge favor. The disruption to the Internet service was caused by a systemwide failure and had nothing to do with the downed cables.

FEBRUARY

AN EXTRAORDINARY ORDINARY DAY

It was an ordinary day. Although it was quite cool in the morning, I knew from the feel of the sun on my face that later in the day, I would happily peel off some layers of clothing. I had been to my yoga class, then reserved a seat for a movie that afternoon. I picked up some wildly expensive fresh organic blueberries and some cheap bananas and tomatoes, then waited for a bus home.

When the bus came, it was very crowded, but with my white hair, yoga mat, and grocery bags, I was offered a seat near the front immediately. As we moved away from the stop, I heard a man on the bus playing a familiar song on his guitar. Men playing guitar on the bus for a few hoped-for pesos from some of the riders is not unusual in San Miguel. I couldn't see him because of all of the standing passengers, but I could certainly make out the words to the John Lennon song "Imagine," which he was singing in English.

I've heard these lyrics hundreds if not thousands of times over the decades, but somehow, I was hearing them for the very first time. It was certainly the first time that I had ever heard them sung in English by a guitar-playing man whom I couldn't see on a bus in Mexico.

As he sang about people without greed or hunger, living in peace and sharing the world, tears gathered in my eyes and spilled down over my cheeks. I was glad for the visor and sunglasses that I'd worn to protect me from the sun's glare while now also partially hiding my face.

I surprised myself by clapping loudly at the end of the song. I was the only one on the bus to do so, perhaps because I was the only one who understood the English words. Soon the guitarist made his way slowly through the standing passengers toward the front of the bus, collecting a few pesos here and there. When he got to me, I gave him 10 pesos and said, *"Me hizo llorar"* (You made me cry).

In reality, Mexico makes me cry time and again. Impunity, corruption, violence, lack of social mobility, insufficient education, food insecurity, very low pay. And yet Mexicans I see in SMA continue on, quite happily I think, although I know that they would prefer more safety and security of all kinds for their families. Faith, family, music, and pride raise them up.

ANGELS AT THE AIRPORT

All the different modes of transportation that I used getting to and from Canada and traveling throughout its east coast on a vacation were fabulous in every way. It made my trip just that much more enjoyable...until we landed at the Mexico City airport, where all was in chaos.

My original plan had been to take a bus from the airport to Querétaro and then change there to another bus to San Miguel. However, when I finally located the ticket office for the buses, a middle-aged Mexican couple were coming up the ramp I was walking down and asked me in Spanish if they could help me. I wondered why they were asking me this, but I told them that I was just going to buy a ticket for the bus to Querétaro. They told me that no buses were able to leave the airport, nor could any other type of transportation come in to drop passengers off or pick them up: no relatives in cars, no Ubers, no taxis, not the bus they and I wanted. There was no way to get to or from the airport in a vehicle.

The couple and I moved away from the ramp and the man, whose name I didn't quite catch, worked his cellphone and found out that it was because of a strike of the National Taxi Movement, for something having to do with Ubers. Shortly we determined that we had been on the same flight from Toronto. They told me that they have a security firm and were there on business. It was clear to me that this was a couple I could trust, and they seemed more than willing to have me join them in the search for a way to get home, they to Querétaro, I to San Miguel.

I could see droves of people walking with their luggage away from the airport, and I asked him what that was about. He said that if you went to the closest *avenida principal* (major street), you could get a taxi there and continue on your way. I figured that you had to be Mexican, know Mexico City, and have the Uber app on your phone, none of which applied to me, in order to do that. There would be no guarantee out on the street that you would get a secure taxi as you would if you used an airport taxi.

I shuddered to think of non-Spanish-speaking people from, say, Singapore, with several little kids, arriving at the scene and not knowing what to do nor where to turn for help. I pictured me having to stay overnight in an airport hotel, and then I thought that many of these people would have to stay overnight in an airport hotel and that there wouldn't be sufficient rooms—and I would wind up waiting in the airport all night long. Not a happy thought.

The male half of my rescuing couple was a take-charge guy. He called for an Uber to meet us on the avenida principal; he secured a porter to take all of our luggage to the street; and he was in constant touch with the Uber driver, which was necessary because we had missed him on his first swing by and he asked him to go around again, taking an amazing amount of time. In total mayhem, we finally got into the Uber of a friendly man named José Luis. Hundreds of people were trying to flag down taxis and family members were trying to meet up with new arrivals, all on a major street. But after José stowed our combined luggage in the trunk, we were on our way to the México Norte bus station, a ride that took at least a half hour in horrendous traffic.

Several times I offered to pay my share of the porter's tip and the taxi ride, but the couple were having none of it. I bought my bus ticket for half price since I have an INAPAM card (a discount card for seniors) and was thrilled to learn that after a short stop in Querétaro, the same bus would continue on to San Miguel. The couple then purchased their tickets to Querétaro, asking for the seats right in front of mine.

We were all starving, and they knew of an *empanada* stall in the terminal. I tried to pay for all of our empanadas, but they wouldn't hear of it. The bus left the terminal half an hour after we got there and we had a pleasant although long ride to Querétaro, where I bid my new best friends a tearful goodbye. After a short stay in the terminal, the bus proceeded to San Miguel, where I caught a taxi, and I reached my apartment safely.

This is the second time in a year and a half that angels in about as different settings and situations as you could ever imagine have appeared to help me at exactly the right moment. I don't know what angels are and I don't believe in the type of angels pictured in a church, but this lovely, helpful, friendly, kind couple were my angels that day. I honestly don't know what I would've done if they had not appeared on that ramp into the bus ticket office at the exact same moment that I did and asked me if they could help me. I know that I would not have been able to find out the information I needed, nor would I have felt secure getting into a taxi alone on the street in front of the airport. I do not know what I would have done without my angels surrounding me, a stranger, with their loving care. I will be forever grateful.

Near the Bitter, Bitter End of 2019

I frequently ride the local city buses, and I have often had interesting experiences on them. But today was different. A migrant—dirty, limping—got on the bus, and as I was very close to the front, I could see that he paid his eight-pesos fare. He then got down on his knees and held the bill of his baseball cap with the round, empty part out in front of him in the well-known posture of a beggar. And in Spanish, of course, he briefly told his story and asked for money for food, even one tortilla, he said. He slowly raised himself and made his way to the back of the bus, still extending the baseball cap. I was happy to see that many on the bus gave him some coins, as did I. And I know that most of those riding the bus have little to spare, and yet they did.

Migrants are in town on a fairly frequent basis, as they walk or ride the tops of the trains from the southern end of Mexico, fleeing violence and poverty in their home countries in Central America, all the way to the border with the U.S., and sometimes they just can't take it anymore and stop off halfway in San Miguel to rest for a while.

Honestly, this country—this world—will tear out your heart and stomp on it every time.

"Es lo que es."
(It is what it is.)
"Es solo una cuestión de aceptación."
(It is only a question of acceptance.)

Wise Mexican advice

CHAPTER 7

2020

SITTING OUT THE PANDEMIC
IN SAN MIGUEL DE ALLENDE

The previous chapter was supposed to be the final one in this book, and then COVID-19 arrived. I decided to add two more chapters to tell about my experiences dealing with it while mostly remaining in San Miguel. Now is a good time to ask once again, Is This My *Life*? As I wrote these chapters starting in late May 2020 and continuing through mid-2021, I have isolated for 20 months. In this time, I've discovered that without a calendar of weekly events I could easily forget which day of the week it is or the date, and, with the weather pretty constant throughout the year in SMA, even the month or season!

EARLY ON

By mid-February 2020, friends had begun to leave San Miguel in droves. The Canadians left early as their provinces ordered them back. In many other cases, it was children in the States who pleaded with their parents to return home as soon as possible, before things got really bad and options were closed to them. Meanwhile, I was hearing from my daughter, Suji, in Philadelphia, that accessing food was becoming quite impossible. Shelves were stripped in supermarkets as people stocked up and hoarded, and there were long lines to get into any kind of food market. She was setting her alarm for midnight or the wee hours of the morning to try to get onto websites that were scheduling delivery times of ordered groceries, but they all seemed to fill up with frightening speed, and orders, when taken and delivered, were sometimes late, incomplete, and wildly overpriced (example—a head of cauliflower for $6.99). I, here in SMA on the other hand, was having absolutely no problem buying anything I needed to eat or drink.

Additionally, Suji and I were apprehensive of a couple of other things: my taking a shared shuttle from San Miguel to León or Querétaro airport, being in three airports and on two planes during the lengthy trip to Philadelphia, and finally having to ride in a taxi from the Philly airport to my apartment. Additionally, the virus had hit Philadelphia very hard. The main center city shopping area just blocks from my apartment was heavily damaged in the political protests gone bad in May 2020, and brought to its knees from the collapse of the local retail and restaurant economy due to COVID. My apartment is on the 14th floor of a building with small elevators. Suji and I agreed that it would be best for me to "shelter in place" in San Miguel.

The SMA government and citizenry response was slow to begin, in my estimation; then, finally, posters on mask use, distancing, and hand-washing appeared. At this time, only about 50 percent of those I saw on the street were mask wearers—zero percent for young, male construction workers and other laborers coming in from the campo, and sure enough, somewhat later, cases developed there. If any of those young men died of the virus, which I certainly hope is not the case, it could be said that they died from machísmo. Even in my own apartment complex, two male ex-pats eschewed mask wearing. After weeks and weeks of very low numbers of infection and no deaths, just around the time that the city was to partially reopen—June 1—our numbers of cases shot up, and two deaths were reported. From that point on, our numbers climbed steadily.

Months before it was a reality, it was announced that all of Mexico, including San Miguel, would see a spike in cases around the end of June and into the first week of July. There were articles about members of the National Guard being a presence at the four street entrances to SMA and the bus station, taking temperatures and names of people coming in and addresses where they'd be staying or proof of reservations at one of the hotels in town. Some have reported that those wearing masks in their cars were waved through; others said they got the full treatment. Who knows what is true?

FOOD AND BEVERAGE

Suji and I collaborated on a list of foods with which to stock my larder against a possible food shortage, including at least two months of non-perishable staples such as rice, pasta, lentils, chickpeas, cooking oil, tuna, mayonnaise, chicken broth, and peanut butter. And because each departing friend quickly got rid of food they couldn't use up before they left town, I was the grateful recipient of quite a haul of goodies: cubed feta cheese, a box of quinoa, an unopened bottle of fancy French jam, several frozen fillets of Alaska wild sockeye salmon from Costco, balsamic vinegar, brown rice, a small bottle of dried Italian herbs, soy sauce, some white wine, and more.

As a person who for years cooked Indian meals from scratch many nights each week for her family of four after returning home from a full day's work, I had overdosed on cooking, and when I was feeding only myself in Philadelphia, I scaled things down considerably, leaning heavily on Trader Joe's interesting, inexpensive, and often organic offerings. When I moved to SMA, I told friends that I no longer cooked; I assembled. I would buy things like homemade pesto, hummus, a variety of soups, a selection of already prepared organic green and vegetable salads, slices of quiche in a number of flavors, Middle Eastern dinners and *pollo* (chicken) wraps with curry mayonnaise, baguettes, bagels, and wedges of some really great cheeses from Luna de Queso, and I would supplement those ingredients with a rotisserie chicken, store-bought pasta and sauce, and granola, among other things. Of course I also bought fresh fruits and vegetables. I could get six or more types of meals from one chicken. I would put many types of toppings on a plate of fusilli, angel-hair pasta, or bow-tie noodles. I didn't have a huge variety of dinners, but as I rotated through 12 to 15 menu items, I was happy and well-nourished.

Using a smart, organized, and punctual university student, Estefanía, to shop for me (and for over 140 other grateful customers) at Costco, about an hour away in the town of Celaya, I added to the list those Alaska wild sockeye salmon fillets and boneless, skinless chicken thighs, better granola, huge plastic bags of frozen organic blueberries, and six-packs of aseptic-packaged almond milk and other items that I used to have to schlep home one by one because of their weight and my dwindling ability to carry much.

Over time alone in my apartment, just for variety's sake and because each meal became a much looked-forward-to part of my day, I became not exactly a cook and certainly not a chef by any means, but I did get a little more experimental. My new go-to food, which, honestly, I could eat daily—and almost do—is chilled cooked quinoa with broccoli florets topped with a creamy cilantro and lime salad dressing that I found at Bonanza. I had never bought it before nor even knew it was available or how magnificent it is. It goes really well on a lot of other foods, too, such as a boiled super-thin-skinned small white potato that I discovered at Gil's Tienda in the nearby *colonia* (neighborhood) of Guadalupe. In my 11 years in SMA, I had never bought a fresh potato to prepare at home.

Now I regularly use those potatoes for home fries and mashed potatoes. And I bought my first bottle of Heinz ketchup to enliven some of those potato dishes.

I buy lentils precooked and sold in a bottle. For one extra-tasty dish, I added some to store-bought pasta sauce into which I mixed some of those dried Italian herbs. I served it all over spaghetti topped with shaved parmesan, and a new dish, which quickly landed high on my list of favorites, was born. The lentils, while incorporating protein, enriched the sauce and made it seem as if it contained meat, which I eat sparingly. I also bought my chickpeas already cooked and in a bottle, and began tossing them into the quinoa and broccoli salad, and oh my, what a rich, toothsome inclusion! And then I slipped some of the gifted feta cheese into the quinoa mix, also, and it just got better and better. Additionally, I put feta into an omelet along with chopped fresh tomatoes and spinach, and another winner came to be.

By happy accident, I discovered that Bonanza carried Costco brand pesto. I was so happy to see this that I almost cried, as Luna de Queso, from which I had been buying its homemade variety for years, had closed down its Calle Jesús location. I adore pesto on fusilli with the addition of some bits of fresh tomatoes thrown in.

I had learned some time ago to buy wine by the case. One gets a big discount for doing that and another for paying cash, which I always do for everything in Mexico; I never use a credit card. And finally, the case is delivered to your door gratis. So, needing a case of my favorite Antares sauvignon blanc from Chile, which I buy every three months or so, one Tuesday I walked to La Europea, a local wine shop that I favor. It was my first time out midday in months, as it is not open when I do my daily early-morning 3-mile walk for exercise. The cash register is near the door and I waited until the previous customer exited before I entered, masked and gloved, to place my order. That was

IS THIS IS MY LIFE?

easily done and delivery was promised for Thursday.

When 5 p.m. rolled around on Thursday, my wine had not been delivered. I couldn't find a phone number on La Europea's website (I had tried on Tuesday, too, unsuccessfully, hoping to order the wine by phone) or anywhere else online, so I went to reception and asked Paco, the chico at the desk that day, to help me. By going deep into the list of sites for La Europea that came up on his screen, he found a phone number and placed the call. After Paco told Felipe (who answered the call) the problem, he learned that Felipe was speaking to him from outside the wine store—as the police had shut it down. We learned that lawyers for La Europea were on their way, that probably the store would reopen the next day, and that I most likely would have my wine on Saturday.

As far as I know, La Europea has been open all the time during the shutdown of nonessential businesses in the city, except for two holidays, one being Mother's Day, when *"ley seca"* (dry law) was in effect so that people would not feel emboldened to have big, boozy parties then. And I had seen some of what I would absolutely not consider essential businesses with their doors open. What was happening? Dare I suggest the word *"mordida"* (bribe)? Anyway, true to Felipe's word, my wine was delivered on Saturday. It is certainly essential for my well-being!

AND ON THE OTHER HAND, LACK OF FOOD

While I wrote above of all the wonderful food I was discovering, buying, preparing, and eating, I thought of the huge number of people who had lost their jobs and the income to support their frequently large families of several generations living under one roof, in a city whose main industry is tourism. They had worked in restaurants and hotels, as taxi drivers and balloon sellers, wedding planners and tour guides, owners of clothing stores, artisans, flower vendors, bartenders, and in other jobs in that sector. Many workers, along with their families, even in the best of times, live a hand-to-mouth existence, eating sufficiently only on those days when they have work and bring in money. The loss of regular income had an immediate, devastating impact.

Now, in the new, locked-down scenario with the barest minimum of tourists, I had scary visions of marauding, starving people in the streets, or the hungry seeing me, a gringa, as a person with money and seeking to relieve me of it. None of those things materialized of course, I'm relieved to say, and certainly one reason has to be that many individuals, both local Mexicans and ex-pats, organizations, and the local government stepped up very quickly to provide *despensas* (larders), bags of nonperishable groceries made available every other week, with items similar to those stocked in my kitchen, in amounts to feed a family of four. Donations of a changing variety of fresh vegetables such as carrots and tomatoes were added to the bags when donated.

Since in many cases the people who most needed the supplies lived in ranchos far out of town and did not have cars or money for a bus to come into Centro to collect the bags, the food was taken to them in trucks. Relying on monetary donations, the operation became huge, extremely well organized, and lifesaving. Feed the Hungry (FTH), for example, which, prior to COVID, had been delivering supplies of food to school kitchens in 37 communities where 4,000 schoolchildren would normally receive a hot meal each day, pivoted, as an emergency response to the closure of the schools, to become Feed the Families, and expanded to include the families of the children, the elderly, and additional families in these communities, serving over 20,000 people. In an emailed letter I received at the end of June 2021, FTH reported that since March 2020, when its program kicked in, ingredients for over 11.5 million meals had been distributed, helping 3,285 families avoid starvation. This cost $1,200,000 USD a year, and each meal came in at only 10 cents USD, totally amazing in my eyes.

So Others May Eat (SOME), which formerly offered a hot lunch once a week in the shadow of the parroquia to elderly Mexicans, switched to bags of food for the same older population, and Amigos al Cien (Friends to the 100), one of the first to identify and help to rectify the food scarcity problem, began by giving provisions to disadvantaged people who made their livings in the center of town, such as the blind and the street musicians. They also sent representatives out of town to search for those with the greatest need, like single mothers. DIF, a national program of social assistance with a branch in SMA, had a program to provide help to the elderly and to families with disabled children. Some colonias organized their own despensa programs, which included vouchers and food essentials, and were designed exclusively for the destitute in their immediate areas.

Many ex-pats, including myself, donated all or part of their stimulus checks to these feeding programs. What a joy it was for me to use that unexpected windfall from the U.S. government to keep Mexicans from going hungry! At the peso equivalent of only $8 to $10 USD per bag of groceries, depending on the amount of canned tuna included, I could see that these donations would go a long way, at least for a while. I am proud to report that my UU congregation in SMA collected and donated $88,000 USD to the feeding programs providing despensas, and individual members supplemented that amount with their own personal gifts.

CITY- AND STATE-FUNDED WORK PROGRAMS

Like the WPA program during the Great Depression in the U.S., but on a much smaller scale, the city government hired close to 3,000 temporary workers from the most vulnerable sectors to participate in the

Renewed Action Program, making more than 300 improvements ranging from streets, roads, and sidewalks to public spaces, educational infrastructure, and stream slopes. Many streets and roads and more than 120 embankments were rehabilitated for water collection. Plus, 150 public squares and sports spaces were upgraded. I was witness to some of these improvements right in my own neighborhood, where sidewalks were repaired and, at the same time, attractive, circular stone protections were built around tree trunks and flowers were planted, and then the adjacent streets were improved.

The state provided the funds to paint more than 1,300,000 square meters of facades, to benefit 25,000 families. And, looking to the future, the first stone was laid for the eventual new home of the San Miguel campus of UNAM, the best public university in the country and one of the most-recognized in the world.

THE MANY KINDNESSES OF THE OWNERS OF CASA DE LOS SOLES

The small, family-owned hotel/apartment complex where I live has 14 units, and during the pandemic, only four were continuously occupied: three by long-term retired gringo renters, including myself, and the fourth by the owners. Their attention to the needs of their guests is always exemplary, but it kicked into high gear at this time of crisis. Because it was believed at that time that COVID could come into one's home on delivered packages or on groceries, co-owner Sandra supplied each of us with spray bottles and three-gallon bottles of disinfecting liquid that she and her staff made up themselves. All of the employees wore masks and gloves at nearly all times, and they had the additional protection of a plastic shield when they came into the apartments to clean. Sanitizing gel was prominent at the reception desk, and a wet disinfecting mat for shoes was installed at the entrance. When the lavanderías closed down temporarily, the Soles staff cheerfully did our personal laundry, not a service it usually offers. When some stores began to reopen, lavanderías followed suit, although with seriously curtailed hours because there was much less demand for their services with so many ex-pats not in town. At that time, I returned to taking my laundry there weekly.

As time wore on and cancellations of reservations for the coming winter months poured in, Soles' owners had to cut their staff. Only one chico remained at reception, trading off occasional days with the owners' son, back in town from his university studies in Puebla, which had gone online. Only one chica per day was needed to keep the small number of occupied apartments tidy. Sandra pitched in often and, for close to three months, I did my own cleaning and changed my sheets and towels weekly, not wanting to infect nor be infected by a housekeeper in my apartment. I guessed that the housekeeper, like the huge majority of other Mexican families, probably lived in a multigenerational household with other members going out to work, possibly without any protections.

When my chronic vertigo of two years resurged, I told Sandra that I didn't think it was wise for me to continue cleaning my place, and I invited the housekeeper back in. Sandra responded by saying that if I needed help of any kind, I was to call her—day or night—as she and her husband are my family in San Miguel. This is a statement not to be spoken or accepted lightly, as family is everything—everything—in Mexico. It's difficult to explain how loved and protected her words made me feel.

CLOTHING

Now that I am in my apartment all day every day, except for my early-morning walk and a speedy in-and-out trip weekly to a small food market at the moment that it opens, a monthly trip to put money on my cell, and an occasional visit to the bank, both of which cannot be done until later in the day, I wear exclusively stretchy pants and T-shirts, formerly reserved just for yoga class, now essential every day for comfort. There was no way I was going to wear street clothes that had to be ironed while being perpetually in the house! The two pairs each of different-length pants and three T-shirts I had were not sufficient to rotate under these circumstances, so I ordered two more pants in the three-quarters length and two more of the full length, as I assumed I'd still be staying at home when fall came. They were received all the way from LL Bean in just under a month, although the shipping and duty fees probably came to more than the cost of the pants themselves. Finding additional T-shirts was more of a challenge, but finally, when stores started to reopen, I found one I liked at one of the tiendas in the artisans' market, steps from my place, and when I ascertained that it did not shrink in the laundry, I returned for another one with a different design on the front.

I had only one pair of earrings that didn't get tangled in the elastic bands of my face masks, and I wore them exclusively from the beginning of the crisis until today, at the end of 2021, as I edit these words, and I imagine that I will continue to wear them and only them until I can at last remove my mask, whenever that may occur.

KEEPING IN SHAPE

While I was staying at home under direction from the SMA city government, it soon became evident that I had to find a way to replace the yoga classes I'd taken in person three times a week and all of the daily walking I used to do just living my life, generally racking up at least 10,000 steps or 4 miles each and every day, but which was now impossible. I decided that mornings are for movement and undertook to walk 3 miles in the "virus quiet" of the early morning, when very few cars or people were on the streets.

San Miguel, on Calle Loreto, keeping watch from his high perch over my neighborhood.

I would start off on my own street, greeting a half-size statue of San Miguel in a high niche of a neighboring house with "Buenos días, San Miguel," said with the same cadence as a similar phrase in the movie *Good Morning, Vietnam.*

Though the jardín was roped off, standards of tree trimming and sweeping were maintained.

I usually wound up at the jardín, which was now off-limits for sitting, and would walk around it numerous times while contemplating it sadly, and up and down the spoke streets leading to and from it.

Of course I continued my daily physical therapy exercises, which I have been doing for over three years, following a bad episode with tendonitis of my hips that came to a head at a family wedding in Telluride, Colorado.

My yoga teacher, Alejandro, who not only had to give up his yoga studio space in a hotel but had to shutter his retail shop and close his catering business, decided to put his beginners, advanced, and restorative yoga classes on Facebook. I helped him write up the notice and sent it out to my large email list and he to his present and past students' group. Members in all groups were located worldwide by then, and adjusting for time zones, could tune in for the classes. I am proud to say that because of this marketing, he started out with 82 paying members! The best part was that you didn't have to do the classes when they were offered live; they were archived and you could do any lesson that you wanted any time of the day or night.

During the first two weeks of May 2020, when we were in a spike period, I decided to curtail my outside walking and instead did an in-home walking video, but it was just too boring and confining, and I returned to walking outside, always masked, of course. Unfortunately, I saw that still about half of those people that I encountered were not masked, and some dodging and weaving took place to avoid getting too close to them.

While doing all of this walking about, I was pleased to see that the Mexicans, who believe that cleanliness is next to godliness, were not letting their standards slip. Most sidewalks in front of homes and businesses were scrubbed each day, as per usual. *Limpias* (cleaning crews) continued their daily sweeping of the streets in El Centro. Trash trucks did not deviate from their thrice-weekly pickup schedule. A parking lot near my apartment was always just opening up as I passed it on my walks, and the man running it was, without fail, sweeping it. I have never seen a cleaner place!

HEALTH AND MEDICATIONS

In all of the years that I've lived here, I have invariably returned to Philadelphia for the months of May, June, and July, and during that time have had all of my annual doctors' and dentist appointments, reordered my medications for the year, and stocked up on the health and beauty aids that I favored and brought them back to SMA with me in my suitcase in August. In 2020, however, that was not an option, so I first canceled all of the appointments that I had made in the beginning of the year for those months and took stock of what I needed to do instead. First, I contacted my physician here, Dr. Roberto Maxwell, and gave him the names and dosages of my few prescriptions to see if those same meds were available in SMA. All of them were, although with different names and presentations.

A happy discovery was that it was cheaper to buy my meds in San Miguel than in the U.S., even with my coverage there of prescription drugs through Medicare. Two friends who returned separately and at different times from the States to SMA each brought me some articles that are not available in SMA, such as U.S. postage stamps and books of checks I ordered and had sent to their homes. This was a huge act of friendship for which I am extremely grateful.

I decided that I would seek help from local specialists for my few problem areas before I could return to the States, especially not knowing how long that might take. As I felt more confident, I made an appointment for my annual checkup with a retina specialist whom I had seen years before. However, I was not yet ready for a haircut until five months later, although heaven knows it was sorely needed! My hairdresser, Miguelina, called me in June to tell me that she had closed her salon where I had been seeing her for over 10 years and had moved to Calle Loreto 26. I almost fainted; I live at Calle Loreto 19!

Next up was outfitting myself in a comfortable cloth face mask. I went through a couple of styles, and when I found one that served me well, I ordered several and kept them washed and in rotation. However, I found that wearing a cloth mask, even for a 3-mile walk, gave me a headache, due to lack of oxygen, I was told, at our high altitude. I mentioned this at my ophthalmologist appointment, fearing that my eyes were somehow to blame, but my doctor reassured me, saying, "You wouldn't believe the headaches that my associates and I have at the end of each workday from wearing masks." I also noticed that I was yawning a lot during the day, which I interpreted as my body's attempt to get more oxygen. Another issue with the masks was that when I really got going on my speed walking, my glasses steamed up. It's tricky enough to maneuver the cobblestoned streets here without having to look at them through foggy lenses. I tried several other styles and materials for my masks, and finally hit on one that didn't give me a headache.

Mask-making became a huge effort in town. Some unemployed seamstresses kept their families going by sewing *cubrebocas* (face masks), prominently displayed for sale at the entrance to many types of stores. Some were magnificently embroidered and carried a high price tag. Many handy locals and ex-pats solicited supplies of material and made masks to be distributed at no cost out in the campo and at other places where mask wearing was not popular for a variety of reasons. I wasn't able to locate medical rubber gloves, as they were in high demand, so I used dishwashing gloves instead when I went shopping.

Calling a face mask a cubreboca has an unfortunate result, since it means "cover the mouth," and a great many Mexicans took that literally and wore them below their noses, possibly infecting others and not doing themselves any favors, either.

AND THEN MY SISTER DIED...

At the end of April 2020, my middle sister, Julia Ruth Claus, died after a valiant, many-years struggle with cancer at her home in Taos, New Mexico, about a month before her 71st birthday. There was no way for members of the family to say good- bye to her in person, and Scott, Julia's partner, was urging

Julia Ruth Claus

us to do something quickly, as Julia was fading fast, so I came up with the idea of doing a Zoom call, which Suji hosted. If that kind of thing can be said to be "successful," well, it was. Our youngest sister, Gretchen, and her spouse, Dave, in Pennsylvania; my son, Ajay, and his wife, Riitta, in Helsinki; Suji and her husband, Geoff, in New Jersey; Julia's son, Dylan, and his partner, Angela, and their two young children, one just a month old, in Washington state; and I, in Mexico, all managed, in our different time zones, to join Julia and Scott for the call. Over one and a quarter hours, we told Julia how much she meant to us and how much we loved her. Scott told us later that that was the longest period of time that Julia had been able to sustain stamina over the previous several weeks. She died peacefully in her sleep a couple of nights later.

VIRTUAL ACTIVITIES

The importance of Zoom and other platforms for the Sunday services, discussion groups, and committee meetings of my UU congregation; for keynote addresses and Poetry and Prose Cafes from the SMA Literary Sala; for author events from the Philadelphia Free Library, Netflix for movies, Kindle for books, and concerts and lectures from a variety of providers cannot be overemphasized. There is the aforementioned yoga on Facebook, and starting in mid-July 2020, I attended a six-week graduate-level poetry-writing class online with much-published author Ellen Bass. Facetime, Skype, and phones with an international reach allowed me to keep in touch with dispersed friends and family members in ways more meaningful than emails, although I also exchanged them in great numbers daily.

KEEPING UP WITH MY SPANISH

Unfortunately, Carlos, my decade-long private Spanish tutor, has a health condition that makes him highly susceptible to COVID, and was advised early on by his doctor that he should stop giving classes in-person and stay in the house 100 percent of the time. To make matters worse, he couldn't even give classes online, as the Internet service in his fairly new development is the world's worst. So I came up with the idea of reading for an hour a day from young-adult books in Spanish to try to keep up my knowledge of the language and even, hopefully, to improve it. I spent many hours perusing the huge list of books in this category on amazon.com.mx, but found that the overwhelming majority of them are romance novels, not my favorite genre. I finally did find four books that looked intriguing and ordered them. The first one I read, *El Otro Lado del Océano (The Other Side of the Ocean)*, was such a huge hit that I sometimes would go past the one-hour mark as I found the story so gripping. I ordered it in the audio version in English for my granddaughter in Helsinki, as I thought that she could relate to the story.

THE ROLE OF MUSIC

Some single friends of mine have told me that mealtimes alone are their greatest challenge, and I can certainly sympathize with that. However, as long as I have music playing while I prepare, eat, and clean up after my meals, I do not miss having another person with whom to share food and conversation, although of course I will welcome that when it is possible. I mostly listen on my iPad to the classical music station I love from my hometown, Philadelphia—WRTI—and am comforted by the familiar voices of the DJs. I also have a small but very eclectic collection of music on CDs and a boom box on which to play them. Whatever my mood on any day, I can usually find something from that collection that will match it and make me happy.

An itinerant violin player, making a stop at the closed-up-tight artisans' market, accompanied by his watchful dog.

A very talented, very handsome young Mexican violin player comes from time to time to the shuttered artisans' market quite close to my apartment and accompanies a full orchestra playing on his portable sound system. Since I always have my windows open in the daytime, I can hear him start up, and I rush outside with some pesos clutched in my hand, which I drop thankfully into his violin case, and then I stand in the shade on the other side of the street and just enjoy his music. He frequently plays many of the most heart-rending numbers you can name, like "Time to Say Goodbye," which always brings me to instant tears. But whatever his repertoire each time, it is remarkable how his half hour or so of musical entertainment raises everyone's *anima* (spirit), as Sandra, co-owner of my apartment complex, once commented when I had to duck back inside during a sudden rain shower.

From my balcony above the street, I could enjoy the members of a mariachi band, a una distancia sana *(at a safe distance), serenading my neighbor on his birthday.*

Our small group of renters was treated to a totally different musical experience at about 9 o'clock in the evening on the birthday of one of us. The owners of our complex had arranged that Bill, my next-door neighbor, be serenaded by a small group of mariachi, masked and properly distanced, with us all looking down from our respective balconies. They started off with the English "Happy Birthday," sang a few old chestnuts in Spanish, and then took requests. It was about 20 minutes of just plain fun.

These few small, friendly musical experiences during this difficult time of collective trauma truly touch my soul and make living here in San Miguel the moving experience that it so often is.

LATER ON

Early in July 2020, the city received the World Travel and Tourism Council's Safe Travels endorsement, and it made sure that all businesses hoping to reopen participated in its Health First certification program to ensure that required health and safety measures were met. Then, on July 15, with our numbers and deaths still steadily climbing, San Miguel reopened to tourists with 40 percent capacity in hotels, which had been closed until then. The hotels would have been thrilled to be at 40 percent occupancy, I think. At first, not that many tourists arrived, as there was really nothing to do here at that time.

With the jardín and Parque Juarez still unavailable, no nightly public entertainment provided by the city, and no music venues permitted to open, the city suggested that visitors choose activities away from Centro, like ATV excursions, horseback riding, or hiking in Charco del Ingenio, the botanical garden, which had just reopened. Restaurants with outdoor seating were permitted to serve customers, or they would be happy to have your order ready for pickup or to deliver it to your home or hotel.

Of course, there is always shopping, and I know that the store owners were glad to see tourists eager to buy after more than two months of not being permitted to open. Speaking of retail, an alarming number of stores went out of business, but within a very short period of time were replaced by others, usually nothing like the ones that had gone under. Renovations to interior spaces could be seen taking place on every block. When I noticed a vaping store going in on a very prominent corner just a block from the jardín, I knew that a new day had come to San Miguel.

The government had several ways in which it hoped to cajole reluctant visitors to wear masks, which included some clever signs.

Also stationed at key points in Centro, such as the artisans' market, were truly hideous blue and white plastic blow-up "sanitizing arches," which emit a fine spray of who knows what as people walk through them. I'm not convinced that they really do any good, but perhaps they suggest to visitors and sanmiguelenses alike that the local government is taking their safety seriously.

I love this no-nonsense poster, which says, "Put it on already!"

Another reminder to wear masks, proclaiming "Obligatory use of masks"
(in this area), was found at gated entries to the streets leading to the jardín.

Is this "COVID-theater" or is it really protecting us from the virus?

FRIENDSHIPS

Of course, one of the main things that for me make San Miguel such an appealing place to live is the close-knit community of friends that I've made—mostly ex-pats, but some fantastic Mexicans, too—and COVID-19 denied me the pleasure of being in their company. We were in frequent touch with one another in any number of ways, no matter where in the world we had chosen or been obliged to be, but of course it is not the same as before.

It's also hard to give up, even if only temporarily, I hope, the enormous array of activities available here: musical performances of every description in a wide variety of venues; lectures and talks on an enormous number of topics; art openings and classes in every medium; movies of amazing variety in funky 20-seat theaters, in larger places, or even at the multiplex at the mall on the outskirts of town; literary events of every stripe including book groups, theater, and play festivals; a number of different worship services and their discussion groups; classes for yoga, water aerobics, dance, singing, computer skills; and much more. I could go on. The offerings are rich and varied, and one is often hard-pressed to fit everything in.

And there's such a cornucopia of restaurant choices: traditional Mexican, modern Mexican, Indian, Thai, Chinese, vegan, Peruvian, pizza, tacos from a street cart, mezcal bars, restaurants with a view, with live music, with loud music, with flirty, fun waiters—it's a paradise of eating choices. Put together, the absence of all three of these elements during the coronavirus pandemic—friends, restaurant meals, and entertainment—and, instead, being forced to be in my apartment alone for months at a time, was a challenge. However, the weather is beyond belief magnificent, and given that there is nothing going on anywhere else in the world, I would rather be where the sun shines each and every day, where the humidity is incredibly low, and where it gets delightfully chilly at night for good sleeping in our little town at 6,500 feet elevation.

My Internet and Mouse Nightmares

I was to have read from *A Lifetime to Get Here: San Miguel de Allende* to a live audience in April for the Literary Sala's monthly Prose Café, but that had to be canceled because of the pandemic. In October, I received an invitation to do that same reading for a virtual audience on Zoom. While I was thrilled, I immediately thought of the sometimes-unreliable Internet service I had where I live and knew that it could very well present problems.

In my first publication about living in SMA, I had quoted from a book of a friend of mine, Carol Merchasin, "Things don't always work in Mexico, but they almost always work out." I feel that it deserves another mention, as it pertains to the following story.

I share the Internet with 13 other apartments, and the complex is certainly not full in these pandemic times, but even under these less-busy circumstances, the Internet can sometimes be really bad. I needed it to be dependable or it was not going to go well for my Zoom reading. I was terrified of it freezing up while I read and ruining the whole program. So I expressed my fears, in Spanish of course, to my landlord, Jorge, and he called in *tecnicos* from Megacable, the company with whom they have the Internet service. They determined after spending a lot of time in my apartment, and even more downstairs in reception talking to Jorge, that the whole place needed a new modem, which they would install gratis, and that would solve my problem.

As English-speaking Cesar, one of the tecnicos, was leaving, he said that they'd be back in three to five days. Great! Then, that night, as I was falling asleep, I realized that in three days, I'd be having a rehearsal with the other two readers at 5 p.m. for our reading on October 1, and in five days would be the actual reading. Just what I needed! So I quickly wrote to Jorge and told him about what I had coming up and when. I did not sleep a wink that night, worrying about this. Jorge replied that I shouldn't worry, as he had everything under control. No details were offered.

That night, pretty late, I got a knock on my door, and Jorge Jr. told me that the festivity *La Alborada* ("the dawn") would take place at 3 a.m. and that fireworks would make a lot of noise for about 10 minutes. Now you have to understand that this is the day to celebrate San Miguel, the patron saint of SMA, and it's usually a huge celebration with thousands of people. Not so this year. Some tourists were in town, of course, but the whole patron saint celebration was going to be virtual except for the shortened version of the La Alborada fireworks. I thanked him for the heads-up. Because of my anxiety about the rehearsal and the iffy Internet, I tossed and turned again that night, but then I must have fallen asleep, because at 4 (not 3, as I was warned, but what's the difference, it was still ghastly early), I was awakened for the 10 very loud minutes of fireworks. Did I rush to the window to see them? I certainly did not. I lay around for a bit more, then got up at 5:50 and did my physical therapy and other things until it got light enough for me to start my walk, which I ended quickly because of drizzle and slippery cobblestones.

At 3 p.m. on the day of my reading rehearsal, with absolutely no warning from anyone (rehearsal was at 5, remember), three tecnicos, including the English-speaking Cesar, showed up from Megacable to give me my very own Internet, not to be shared with anyone. This was wonderful news, but I had no idea that that was the plan. I told them that I had the rehearsal in just two hours and that they must be finished well before 5 p.m. Not a problem, I was told; they'd be in and out in an hour.

Much discussion ensued among the young men about where to put my modem, and then when we were all in agreement, they drilled a hole in the wall under a desk that I don't use and brought my Internet cable in from the street and set my modem up on the unused desk. And they were out by 4, as promised ("…things usually work out"). Whew!

I recovered for a half an hour and then got ready for the rehearsal. I met the two other readers, and we adjusted our sound, light, and position on the screen, learned to respond to the cues we were told about, did a mini-reading, and then gave our cue to the host that we were finished. And all of this with no sleep! I felt such relief when it was over.

Two days later, at the Prose Café, I was the second reader, after Angie Abdou, and I had a computer mouse issue just before she started to read. When it was my turn, I needed a working mouse to click on my manuscript hiding behind the Zoom screen on my laptop and to scroll it down as I read from it. I had checked the mouse earlier in the day and it was 61 percent charged, but it had gone out on other occasions for no discernable reason, and that had given me yet another thing about which to worry as I lay awake at night. That day, the mouse just would not reconnect after it disconnected, no matter what I did. While Angie read, I dashed to my office and got fresh batteries (I'd been set up for the read-ing at my dining room table), and it took forever for it to reconnect, or so it seemed, but it finally did, just in time for my reading. I had my paper manuscript ready off to the side as a backup plan that I really didn't want to use. I had an excellent reading that night, but what a lot of sleepless-ness, anxiety, and hard work for 10 minutes of "fame." Guess that's what it takes, but I couldn't do that very often. I'm sure that I aged a decade.

END AND BEGINNING OF THE YEAR CELEBRATIONS

At this point in the pandemic, almost-universal mask-wearing could be observed because by this time in our small town almost everyone proba-bly knew someone who had been sick with COVID or even died from it, and when well-known local people succumbed, their deaths were prom-inently written up in the city papers.

A dear friend, Rachel, moved to an apartment complex literally steps from mine, and when she had settled in, we made arrangements for the occasional get-together for wine and nibbles on her outdoor terrace or mine while following protocols. I invited her for Christmas *comida* (midday meal) and for the first time since COVID began, ordered de-livery from a restaurant, in this case an Italian place located between our two homes. I also bought a chocolate tres leches cake for dessert from a very popular bakery around the corner, and she brought bubbly. After our truly memorable meal, we played our own rendition of Bananagrams and chatted, and the afternoon soon turned to evening.

At that meal, we made arrangements to celebrate an early New Year's Eve together a week later, complete with a vegetarian pizza delivered from the next street over, ordered in a size large enough to enable us each to have extra slices left over for other meals, with ice cream for dessert.

Finally, a week after that, on January 6, Three Kings' Day, Rachel and I again ordered from the Italian restaurant, finishing the meal with slices of the special sweet, celebratory bread of the day, rosca de reyes. Again we had a relaxing, fun time just talking; she showed me the improvements and changes to her new abode and artwork that she had recently hung.

And thus I bid farewell to a difficult 2020, with hopes for a better 2021 for all on our hurting planet.

"Throw your dreams into space like a kite,
and you do not know what it will bring back, a new life,
a new friend, a new love, a new country."

Anaïs Nin

CHAPTER 8

2021

AND THE COVID BEAT GOES ON...

I turned to a fresh calendar for the new year, the world's second in the clutches of COVID. I had to laugh at the idea of even needing a calendar. I certainly hadn't done 99 percent of my usual activities in the last nine months of 2020, and I had little hope of returning to any of them in the new year. And yet, I looked at the blank page for January and hoped for the best.

JANUARY

IN SEARCH OF THE VACCINE

As a very cold January in SMA moved toward its midpoint, I began to think seriously of taking my leave for the time it would take me to get the two COVID-19 shots, and that meant a return to Philadelphia. It had been more than a decade since I'd been there in the winter, and the prospect of February in Philly was not at all a happy one, but I felt that it had to be done. I didn't see any progress locally in getting shots administered, and I honestly didn't have faith in the infrastructure of Mexico to enable maintaining the vaccine at a sub-subzero temperature for a sustained period of time and while in transit, as was necessary for some brands. So, on January 24, I flew to my hometown. Now it was my turn to give away food that I couldn't eat before my departure date. I set my return date as June 1, not having any idea how long it would take me to procure the vaccine.

The arrangements that I made to protect myself on that all-day trip brought to the forefront my awareness of the great privilege that I have in being able to organize and pay for special accommodations: I ordered a private, rather than a shared, shuttle from my SMA apartment to the León airport, and was picked up in a 10-passenger van for just the driver and myself. I could sit about two-thirds of the way back, keeping a good distance between us. He was masked and I wore both a mask and a plastic face shield, and he had several windows open for circulation of air. For the only time in my life to date, I flew first-class, changed planes in Dallas/Fort Worth, and continued on to Philadelphia. When I arrived at my apartment at about 11 p.m., I showered and washed my hair and put all my clothes and my cloth backpack into the washing machine.

A friend in my building told me she and her husband had already had their first shots from a local chain pharmacy, but my city had badly bungled the rollout of the vaccine, and I didn't see anything too promising on the horizon. However, the manager of my apartment complex got us tenants, overwhelmingly seniors, registered with an independent pharmacy for second-in-line vaccines right after medical and front-line workers. A unique plan for administering the shots allowed us all to stay in our apartments, maintaining distance from other tenants and not having to bundle up and stand in long lines in bitter cold, as I'd heard was happening. I signed up immediately, and exactly one month from the day I arrived in Philly, I got my first shot, with the second one three weeks later. I killed time awaiting the shots by going to a number of overdue doctors' appointments, sometimes walking an unbelievable distance to them as I didn't want to use public transpor-tation; recording as an audiobook the first title in my SMA series, *A Lifetime to Get Here: San Miguel de Allende*; working on my taxes; and Zooming into a lot of programs, classes, and events.

FEBRUARY AND MARCH

IT'S TRUE: YOU CAN'T GO HOME AGAIN

Still making efficient use of my time in the States, I bought a new laptop to replace my 2013 model and struggled mightily and to the point of exhaustion to get up to speed with an operating system that was quite a few versions above the old one. With my new lens prescription in hand from my ophthalmology appointment, I shopped for new glasses, and doing so during a pandemic was quite the experience. One had to make an appointment to enter the optical shop, and after glasses were tried on, they went into one of two baskets: "rejects," to be sanitized by an employee and replaced on the shelf for the next customer to consider, and "possibles," to be carried around until a decision was made and a final choice purchased.

On another outing, I replaced some shoes that had given their all walking the cobbled streets of San Miguel. And in doing all of this walking and shopping in the thoroughfares around my apartment, I got a chance to see, up close and personal, the center of the city into which I was born and where I grew up, raised my family, and worked and lived happily and proudly until I moved to San Miguel. It was not a pretty sight.

The majority of the destruction resulting from the civil unrest of May 2020 took place in a high-quality shopping area about three blocks from my apartment, and the pandemic-induced retail and restaurant collapse pretty much finished it off. Many store windows remained bro-ken, covered by hastily installed boards that were by now scrawled with graffiti. About every third or fourth store was abandoned, some with merchandise still on tables and racks, others cleaned out to the walls. The stores that remained open were empty, and clerks stood at counters on their cellphones, killing time until closing.

When I discovered all this, it was a bitter cold and windy day in February on which I had to maneuver over dirty piles of snow and scary patches of ice while noticing frequent signs on the sidewalk warning of ice falling from tall apartment buildings. But the most upsetting thing was the legion of homeless people, many with mental problems, wandering around carrying their belongings in plastic bags, some ranting, some begging, all looking cold and miserable. As the weather warmed over the next month, some homeless could be found sleeping over sidewalk grates or in doorways.

Other things had changed, too. Many items I needed in my local drugstore were now under lock and key, including such pedestrian products as toothpaste. One had to ring a buzzer, and an announcement could be heard in the nearly empty store that a customer required assistance in the dental products aisle, but no one came after repeated buzzing. After being used to the slow speed of cars and trucks in SMA navigating cobblestoned streets, I found that traffic in the city flew by dangerously, and in fact, on one stretch where I liked to walk away from the hustle and bustle, a runaway car had earlier come over the curb, taking down five saplings and a light post and churning up a lot of grass and dirt before finally coming to a halt. Countless motorcycles, off-road vehicles, and cars and trucks lacking proper mufflers, with no one stopping and ticketing them, roared through the empty nighttime streets, sending up unimaginable noise in the canyons formed by the high-rise buildings, awakening thousands of people in their apartments when sleep was a precious pandemic commodity.

A short trip to a crowded Whole Foods one Saturday showed me that youth culture was in the ascendancy, that technology ruled, and that move 'em in and get 'em out was the name of the game. Then there were the crime statistics, so out of control it was heart-wrenching to realize it could be true. The sale of guns was way up, and the use of them and the resulting homicides broke all records. Carjacking was an everyday occurrence. I withdrew from the scene; it was all too painful for me and I needed to go back to Mexico, quickly. And I did, in early April, a few days after Easter, as I assumed by then that the visiting tourists in San Miguel would have returned home.

Back in SMA, I didn't hear my neighborhood *elote* (corn on the cob) man for a long time, shouting out the names of his wares in his unique fashion, and I worried that he had COVID or had even died from it. After a while, another elote man came on the scene, but his cry was a weak echo compared to No. 1. After a long time, I was thrilled to hear the original purveyor's signature cry, and I rejoiced.

APRIL

SAN MIGUEL AFTER THE PANDEMIC

It is my strong belief that after the pandemic is over, in who knows how many months or even years, San Miguel will be different. I don't think it will be the SMA I wrote about in *Lifetime* or even in the earlier chapters of this book. It will still be magical. It was before I found it and will continue to be when I'm gone. A new generation of sanmiguelenses will shape it to their image and a new crop of ex-pats will discover and fall in love with it. But it won't ever be the same as I loved it, just as was true of the city of my birth. Of that I am sure.

And when I think to my future, I believe it will be spent in San Miguel, as my foray to Philadelphia showed me that it had very much lost its luster, that everything there was too fast for me now, and that compared to the slower, more manageable, more human-scale pace I enjoy in

SMA, I was out of my depth and not at all comfortable there anymore. Who would have guessed that I'd be blissfully happy confining my life to about a one-mile radius in a small colonial town in the mountains of central Mexico.

MAY

LESSONS FROM THE PANDEMIC: I COUNT MY BLESSINGS AND WISH THERE COULD BE A VACCINE FOR POVERTY

I became ever more aware of and worried about not only those in poverty around me, but of the millions of people the world over, who are desperately suffering because of the pandemic, layered on top of pre-existing poverty and all that that entails, lack of or inferior education, dearth of opportunities to better their condition, entrenched sexism and racism, climate change, and the list goes on. I became sharply aware of my enormous privilege as a white woman from the U.S. in excellent health, with a fine education and resources, including the ability to pick up and leave on my terms in order to find the vaccine, and then return. I also rethought my reaction to the rather harsh discipline under which I was raised, finding that it served me well in the lifestyle I was forced to undertake along with everyone else during the pandemic, in terms of continuing with exercise and other good bodily habits, such as diet, and keeping my mind active and working hard on a number of fronts, including creating my books about living in SMA.

JUNE

THE JARDÍN REOPENS!

On Wednesday, June 16, the long off-limits jardín reopened! The families returned! I discovered the reopening during my early-morning walk when all the iron barriers were removed and only one couple sat inside drinking coffee. I asked the obvious question, *"Está abierto el jardín?"* And when they answered joyfully in the affirmative, I started to cry. It was wonderful to see this expression of normalcy after 15 months of closure. When I returned later in the day to take some photos, lots of people were enjoying ice cream cones, chatting happily with one another, taking photos of themselves in front of the parroquia, soaking up the sun, and otherwise exalting in the return to the way things used to be at their beloved gathering place, the jardín, San Miguel's living room.

And early Saturday night, as I walked to meet a friend at a restaurant, whom should I encounter but several troupes of mariachi heading to the jardín with their instruments, most with huge grins on their faces! And no wonder. They could play tourists' favorite songs again, and they could supplement the pay from their day jobs, if they still existed, while having a joyous time.

JULY

SHARED NATURE EXPERIENCE

If I ever had any doubt, which I never have, that San Miguel de Allende is the place for me, it was reaffirmed one late-July morning. I was up early, after just having returned from a week at the beach in the U.S. with my family, to take my dirty clothes to the lavandería and to do some grocery shopping.

As I rounded the corner near my casa, I saw three tiny birds flying haphazardly right in front of me. At the same moment, the man who runs the parking garage there—someone I see almost every morning as I start my daily walk, a Mexican in his early 50s who speaks English to me since he spent many years in the U.S.—came running out giddily, shouting, "Did you see them? Did you see them? They are flying for the first time!" He pointed to the top of the structure that allows the huge garage door to open and shut, where two tiny ones still quivered on a nest's edge, not quite ready to fledge yet. He said with a huge smile, "I am so glad to have been able to share this moment with you!"

I agreed. I watched with him as the brave three, still flapping their wings wildly, tried to keep their balance on a telephone wire, then I exchanged another smile with this person whose name I don't even know, nor he mine, and continued on my way.

As I returned by the same route about 30 minutes later, he was still standing at the entrance to the garage, and I asked him if the two had flown yet. He said no, then pointed out the mother bird, keeping an eye on her fledglings but also occasionally bringing a tidbit to eat back to the two still in the nest. We watched and smiled at each other again. The perfect beginning to my first day back.

These are the kinds of moments I would share with my family, in fact, did share with my family on our recent beach trip. Having heard a report, we walked a long way on the packed Jersey sand near the ocean's edge to see some stingrays trapped in a large pool of seawater created by some boulder barriers; the rays would not be able to get back into the open ocean until it was again high tide. We watched for passing dolphins at a time when they usually swim and cavort to who knows what destination, and we looked on in awe at a feeding frenzy when thousands of seabirds congregated right before our eyes in a spot in the ocean where there was obviously a large school of the type of fish they eat. And certainly a highlight was all of us sitting together on the deck to watch the full moon rise and rise and rise, eventually casting its light in a long golden swath over the ocean.

These and other shared experiences, no matter how small, are the moments that bring me great joy, whether in a parking garage in the high desert town of San Miguel in Mexico or at the beach in New Jersey, U.S.A., and I treasure them.

※ ※ ※

EPILOGUE

A RETURN TO THE QUESTIONS I POSED IN LIFETIME

In the Prologue to my earlier book about my adopted home in Mexico, *A Lifetime to Get Here: San Miguel de Allende*, I asked myself if the early trips in which my father took the family to Mexico planted the seeds for my late-in-life return to it and embrace of it. And my answer is resoundingly yes. I believe that on those trips, for the first time in my life I was able to see that there was a different way to live, fresh places to explore, novel cultures, the unfamiliar but appealing sounds of an unknown language, and untried ways of doing things. It might even be part of the reason that I fell in love with, married, and had a family with a man from India!

My father did a lot of things wrong in my upbringing, but opening the door and introducing my mind to exotic possibilities, strange lands, and unique ways of being has turned out to be a gift, perhaps his greatest, and I thank him for it.

※ ※ ※

"We write to taste life twice, in the moment and in retrospect."

Anaïs Nin

ACKNOWLEDGMENTS

With this book, I bid adiós to my amazing team of more than six years: editor Dulcie Shoener and cover and book designer Margot Boland. Together we have brought four of my books to publication. Our triumvirate—"a group of three powerful or notable people...existing in relation to each other," which describes us perfectly, I think—has been through a lot together, both in the work and personally, during these years. From the beginning, we divided up our duties almost effortlessly, as we each understood where our strengths and expertise lay in relation to the others in the creative, collaborative process.

Thank you both for your attention to detail, your partnership, your deep knowledge of your respective specialties, your good humor, your humanity, and your always-helpful suggestions in the service of my words and photos.

It has been a fun and exciting ride for me. I hope the same is true for you both.

A shout-out to Jayne Halle, for her sensitive and flattering photos of me on two of my books' covers and inside pages.

And finally, a huge vote of thanks to all the hundreds of people who bought and loved *A Lifetime to Get Here: San Miguel de Allende* and who took the time to tell me so and to add that they couldn't wait for this sequel. Well, for you, here it is at last!

ABOUT THE AUTHOR

Is This My Life? *San Miguel and Beyond* is Cynthia's fourth book in five years and is the second in the two-book series Contemplating Inexplicable Mexico. These volumes tell of her adventures: first, visiting San Miguel de Allende (SMA) for longer and longer periods of time over a span of four years, 2009-12 (*A Lifetime to Get Here: San Miguel de Allende*), then selling her home in Philadelphia and moving to that colonial town in the mountains of central Mexico (2013-present). In both books, Cynthia's evocative photos complement the narrative.

Cynthia's first book, *An Orchid Sari: The Personal Diary of an American Mom in 1960s India*, was published in 2017. In 1968-69, on a nine-week trip with her Indian husband and their two-year-old son to India to present themselves to Suresh's relatives for the first time, Cynthia meticulously kept a travel diary and wrote frequent aerograms to family and friends back home, which they saved for her. Close to the occasion of her son's 50th birthday, these resources, plus photos from the trip, saw the light of day and became the material for that book. Her next book, *Ice Cream & Pretzels and Other Stories: A Memoir*, 17 vignettes and a poem, came out a year later.

In 1965, Cynthia received her B.A. degree in English from Temple University in Philadelphia. Following her stint as a full-time mother, all of Cynthia's employment was with nonprofits in Philadelphia: after working with her neighborhood community organization and at an alternative school, Cynthia was employed for 13 years at a seminary, retiring as administrative assistant to the president for publications. In retirement, Cynthia taught English as a Second Language (ESL) as a volunteer for 14 years to adult immigrants.

Praise for Cynthia's first title in this series, *A Lifetime to Get Here: San Miguel de Allende*

"Buy the book. I got mine from Amazon. It's like sitting with a dear friend who's telling you her adventures from childhood to now! You don't want the visit to end! It's funny, heartwarming and so real."

"This is a great book full of experiences that any newcomer would want to know about—funny and chatty, a joy to read. Bravo, Cynthia!"

"A blueprint for a single woman: how to start living and be happy in San Miguel de Allende."

"Highly informative and accurate account."

"What an amazing book, packed full of enjoyment and information."

"Most authentic, enjoyable, remarkable!"

"If you've been there, you can relate. If not, pack your bags!"

"*A Lifetime to Get Here* is such a perfect title for her book, and in every page you can feel just how much the city has grown in her heart. Reading it transported me back to San Miguel, as I'm sure it would anyone who has been there. Moving from one culture to another is a challenge, one which Cynthia wholeheartedly embraced. Her book is filled with everyday experiences, history, Mexican culture and festivals, and a great deal of feeling. Thank you for taking us on your adventure!"

"A great guide to life in SMA for both newcomers and even us old hands! I highly recommend!"

"Your book is one of the best inspirational books about SMA I have read. I read it and reread. I'm two weeks away from moving to SMA and your book couldn't come at a better time for me. Thank you."

"Something warm and inviting about this book."

"A friend of mine who was visiting SMA 'borrowed' my book and took it back to the U.S. because she couldn't put it down!"

"Cynthia's book *A Lifetime to Get Here* is an invaluable resource for anyone considering moving to San Miguel. Beautifully written, it is chock full of interesting places and events that happen here. Any doubts I had about moving here disappeared after reading her book."

"Cynthia's book is a delight to read. I learned things about living in SMA that I didn't know even though I've lived here for 10 years."

"Your book is a joy."

"Very good read for San Miguel newbies or oldies."

"I listened to your book on Audible and loved it. The stories were wonderful and I learned so much."

"It's great! I've been coming here for 20 years and still learned a lot from this book."

"I'm reading it now, and find so much familiarity, and sometimes hilarity, having been here myself, through so much of your experiences. A fun read."

"I just have to tell you that I am homesick for SMA…You brought back so many memories and reminded me of what I'm missing."

"How lucky you are to have been able to follow your dream. You read with such enthusiasm that I want to pack a bag, buy a ticket, and follow your path."

"This book was so enjoyable that I was sorry when I came to the end of it."

"I just got to SMA and I listened to your book on the drive down from Wyoming. I enjoyed it very much and was better prepared to navigate when I arrived."

"I recommend this book for readers who look for a clear-eyed walk through a life of adventure, challenges, and joy. By documenting her choice to upend her life in the States and settle in a strange, new world … Cynthia has shared intimate details that we can all somehow relate to."

❁ ❁ ❁

You might also enjoy Cynthia's earlier books:

An Orchid Sari: The Personal Diary of an American Mom in 1960s India

Ice Cream & Pretzels and Other Stories: A Memoir

CONSIDER DONATING TO THESE WORTHY SMA NONPROFITS!

Below are the nonprofit organizations in San Miguel that I have supported in one way or another over the years and about which I have written in my books about SMA. They are all worthy of your time, talent, and treasure, and I urge you to check out any that are of particular interest to see how you might add your gifts of all kinds to help the deserving Mexicans that they serve. Thank you very much!

CAMINAMOS JUNTOS (WE WALK TOGETHER)

CJSMA.ORG

"The mission of Caminamos Juntos is to provide the necessary accompaniment and comprehensive services to the Mexicans who have been deported from the U.S. and their families who accompany them, who do not have a solid local support network and need help to integrate into the community of San Miguel de Allende."

CEDESA

THE AGRICULTURAL DEVELOPMENT CENTER

(NO WEBSITE AT THE TIME OF THIS WRITING)

A Civil Society organization with more than 50 years of work that contributes to the integral development of the peasant and Indigenous communities of the Independencia Basin, through processes of promotion, organization, and training aimed at strengthening their identity, as well as their capacities for knowledge, analysis, and autonomous decision-making to face and transform in an organized way the situations that affect the lives of people and communities.

CENTER FOR GLOBAL JUSTICE

GLOBALJUSTICECENTER.ORG

A multicultural, democratically organized service, learning, and research center that seeks to empower ordinary people to work to create a more socially and economically just world. It sponsors public education events as well as travel to Cuba, Chiapas, and cooperatives.

EL CHARCO DEL INGENIO

ELCHARCO.ORG.MX

A botanical garden and nature preserve that boasts sculptures, industrial ruins, cultural and artistic spaces, and an endorsement from the Dalai Lama as a "Peace Zone."

FEED THE HUNGRY

FEEDTHEHUNGRYSMA.ORG

Committed to improving the health and well-being of the children of SMA by alleviating hunger through school meals, family nutrition education, and community development programs.

HOUSE AND GARDEN TOURS OF THE BIBLIOTECA PÚBLICA

LABIBLIOTECAPUBLICA.ORG

The public library provides a vital and inviting community center that offers a lending library, skills training, and educational and cultural activities in a safe environment for a multigenerational and multicultural community. The House and Garden Tours are one of the several creative and supportive ways in which the library is funded.

LATIN AMERICAN RELIEF FUND (LARF)

LATINAMERICANRELIEFFUND.ORG

The mission of this NGO is "to support humanitarian organizations that assist migrants and refugees in Mexico, including Albergue ABBA shelter in Celaya, Guanajuato. LARF seeks to raise awareness about the plight of migrants fleeing poverty, violence, and the consequences of climate change."

MUJERES EN CAMBIO (WOMEN CHANGING)

MUJERESENCAMBIO.ORG

This organization, run by volunteers, is committed to enhancing the lives of women living in the rural communities near San Miguel de Allende. Scholarships from Mujeres en Cambio enable rural girls to continue their education beyond grade school. Completing their education will enhance their independence and help break the chain of poverty for them and their families.

OJALÀ NIÑOS

OJALA-NINOS.ORG

Year-round extracurricular classes in arts, crafts, music, literacy, and more for 100 Indigenous students in the rural community of San Miguel Viejo.

Patronato Pro Niños

PATRONATOPRONINOS.ORG

"Saving Lives: Every Child. Every Year." Its mission is to provide high-level medical, dental, and psychological care to children and adolescents from economically deprived families in the municipality of San Miguel.

PEN International

PEN-INTERNATIONAL.ORG

PEN operates in 115 countries and stands for the principle of unhampered transmission of thought within each nation and between all nations.

Pro Música San Miguel de Allende

PROMUSICASMA.ORG

Making a positive difference in the cultural life of SMA and helping young musicians fulfill their potential experience by providing a world-class season each year of concerts and opera as well as funding an extensive educational outreach program for children and young adults.

SMA Literary Sala/Writers' Conference

SANMIGUELLITERARYSALA.ORG

"Connecting You to the World of Writing."

The Sala's goal since its inception in 2004 has been to create a lively writing and reading community by producing bilingual events such as the San Miguel Writers' Conference and the Distinguished Speakers Series. Online workshops, lectures, and other events are expanding the community from SMA to the world.

So Others May Eat (SOME)

SOOTHERSMAYEAT.ORG

Its mission is to serve a weekly hot nutritious meal in an attractive, fun, informative, and respectful way to elderly patrons of limited means.

The Unitarian Universalist Fellowship of San Miguel de Allende

UUFSMA.ORG

"Our mission is to serve the spirit as each individual understands it, to serve the educational and pastoral needs of our own community, and to serve our multicultural community through actions that further social justice."

❈ ❈ ❈

Over the years, I have supported other NGOs that didn't make it into my books. They are all equally deserving, and I ask you to look them over also, and support them in whatever ways you feel called upon.

Caminos de Agua

CAMINOSDEAGUA.ORG

"Caminos de Agua believes that access to safe, healthy drinking water should be a fundamental human right. Our mission is to improve human health and community well-being through adequate and affordable access to clean water."

CASA

CASA.ORG.MX

CASA attends to young people with health and education services including a maternity clinic, a midwifery school, a child development center, a sexual health education program, a program to support vulnerable groups of women subject to gender and domestic violence, a library program, and more.

CASITA LINDA

CASITALINDA.ORG

"Building hope one house at a time. ... Casita Linda helps families in the greater San Miguel area who have an income of less than $300 USD ($6,000 MXP) per month build their own homes. By providing a dignified and safe environment—a *casita linda* or pretty little home—we empower families and change lives. We support our communities by offering workshops on health, family planning, family communication skills, water conservation and other important topics. Families are turning their lives around, building from the foundation of a safe, secure home."

ESCUELA DE EDUCATIÓN ESPECIAL

EEESMA.COM

"Our mission is to ensure that all San Miguel de Allende children who are Deaf become literate, independent, and productive citizens who set and achieve life goals."

JÓVENES ADELANTE

JOVENESADELANTE.ORG

"Jóvenes Adelante unlocks a radically more expansive future for the youth of Mexico by easing financial barriers to higher education, while simultaneously developing their life and leadership skills. We're a nonprofit organization that gives scholarships and opportunities to economically disadvantaged San Miguel de Allende youth in pursuit of higher education. We provide monthly financial support, mentors for personalized support, loan of a laptop, workshops to develop life skills, as well as professional psycho-pedagogical assistance, English tutoring, and a network of graduates."

LIBROS PARA TODOS

SANMIGUELLITERARYSALA.ORG/
COMMUNITY-PROJECTS

Libros para Todos is an organization under the umbrella of the San Miguel Literary Sala that is a registered Association Civil (AC) in San Miguel de Allende. "Libros para Todos' mission is to inspire children to read more and enjoy reading. We focus our efforts on children from families of limited means in rural communities where access to books is much more limited."

Made in the USA
Middletown, DE
10 December 2022

17592442R00115